Gamhanan: English to Cebuano Translation 101

A No-Brainer Guide To Translating Complex English Terms And Phrases Into Cebuano (Visayan) Dialect

KD Sofia Sigil

Dedication

This book is dedicated to all beginners who have found inspiration in learning and understanding the Cebuano (Visayan) dialect.

I intended this book to be a serving of inspirational translated phrases for you.

I intended this book to be your thought-provoking immersion into the Cebuano (Visayan) words.

I intended this book to get you engaged in the literary merit and the richness of the spoken Visayan language.

I intended this book to be your own superpower in tackling the Cebuano (Visayan) dialect.

I intended for you to be a self-professed, "Gamhanan!" to acknowledge your mastery in deciphering the meaning in words, from Cebuano (Visayan) dialect to English language and vice versa.

I hope that the learning that you gain from this material will be timeless.

That the knowledge that you acquire from this resource will survive new ideas, new technologies, new words.

To my favorite elementary English teacher, Mrs. L. Rebollos,
thank you.

To Danielle, Kate and Sofie,
this labor of love is for all three of you.

Preface

This sequel to the first book that was published, *BisDak: Learn to Speak Cebuano Overnight*, is created to provide you, the learner, a comprehensive platform that will speed up your concerted efforts of learning the spoken Cebuano or Visayan dialect.

Let us presume that you came to Cebu and the neighboring islands initially thinking that you were here just for a vacation. Then you fell in love with the city, the language, its culture and its people. You then decided to include Cebu as one of your domiciles. And the rest is history.

This book will guide you in dissecting the Cebuano language in many ways possible. Compare it to attempting to kill a cat with nine lives, not that you would want to kill a cat, but to hypothetically understand the many ways you can decode the most common Cebuano phrases.

What sets this book apart from any Cebuano language tutorial? This book will try to get down to the bottom of things. A deep immersion into English to Cebuano translation will be tackled such that by the end of this book you will have a general mastery of the most common spoken phrases in Cebuano (Visayan) dialect and its English equivalent. This material will also touch on how clauses can be rearranged without ruining the context of the phrase or statement.

And more importantly, this language resource offers a rich compendium, a treasury of Cebuano and Visayan learning that you won't find in any other Visayan tutorial book.

The author of this writing lived and breathed the Visayan language for a good thirty some years of her life, being born and raised in the Philippines. She is equally literate in Tagalog, the other spoken language of the Philippines. And her third language of fluency is the American English language.

Like the first book on speaking Cebuano (Visayan) language, this writing and form of teaching will be totally unstructured but will be essentially enlightening in terms of decoding a pattern of the speech the way the language is captured in the streets of Cebu and the neighboring Visayan islands.

But unlike the first publication, this material will delve a little deeper into the Cebuano (Visayan) dialect. It will be a challenging feat but worry not. With a skilled driver on deck, we can take a smoother ride along the few learning hurdles.

If you are a beginner, the teachings in this book might be a little too overwhelming for you. I suggest that you expose yourself to a quick tutorial of the basic Cebuano (Visayan) dialect. Check out, BisDak: Learn to Speak Cebuano Overnight, the first Visayan tutorial by the same author.

After finishing this book, you will gain an appreciation of the richness and functionality of the Visayan language. You will be armed with a weaponry of witty words and phrases that embody the Philippine culture as a whole.

If there's one quick knowledge you need to assimilate at this point, the diversity of the culture has spanned different influences. Visitors are now coming not only from the Americas and the EUs. There is now a massive input of visitors from the Far East; adjacent neighbors who speak a totally different variety of Southeast Asian languages. Tourists coming from Korea, Japan, China, India, breeze in and out of the islands in multitudes. A few of them have relocated, settled down, or established business partnerships and residencies in Cebu and the Bisaya-speaking islands.

With this, more and more diversity is created, and the evolution of the language expressly embodies that fact. It's not surprising to hear words that are concocted from two words that are not pure Visayan in origin. This tutorial however, will stick to Cebuano (Visayan) words as much as possible.

On occasion, exceptions can be made, when certain words have no Cebuano translation. Some words are not translated when they don't practically make the use of the language more functional or more accessible to the speaker or the listener.

Translation of such kind will be discussed when we do come across certain words or phrases as outlined.

In the later part of this book, we will tap into the age of technology and will play with some social media and internet terminologies and find out 'how much bite we have in our bark.'

Are you ready? Put your genius hat on. We're on to some in depth Cebuano language learning adventure.

Contents

Dedication 2
Chapter 1 9
How Much of A Visayan Are You? 10
    Furrowed Brows for The Morrow 10
    'In Da Haus' Lingo 11
    Not Lost in Translation 14
Chapter 2 18
Say It Like A Cebuano 19
Chapter 3 21
Get to Know The Basics 22
    Basic Visayan Words That You Need to Understand 22
    Negation 26
    Basic Sentence Construction 28
    Rearranging Phrases 31
    The Plural Form 34
    The Root of Words 35
Chapter 4 38
Conjunctions And More 39
Conventions You Need to Know And Learn 44
    The Shortened Form of Words (Cebuano vs Visayan) 44
    Cebuano with 'w' instead of the Visayan 'l' 45
    Same Word, Different Meanings 45
Chapter 5 47
Speak Up: English to Cebuano 48
    50 Phrases You Need to Master 48
Chapter 6 55

Translation 101 56
    Framing the Subject 56
    El Niño Mi-sutoy! 60
    The Verb Tenses 61
    Familiarize Yourself With These Common Prefixes 63
    Did You Know This? 67

Chapter 7 70
Immersion Into the Cebuano (Visayan) Language 71
    Challenge Your Comprehension 71
    Be Curious 72

Chapter 8 74
Functionality in Translation 75
Chapter 9 82
Aspire to Translate to Inspire 83
    Say It Differently, But Say It Right 83
    More Practice Translations 86
    Mastery Thru Practice 88

Chapter 10 90
When All Else Fails, Translate! 91
    Will you pass the challenge? 91
    Ka-ubo! 93
    Gi-sunggo! 94
    Balik-Lantaw (A Look Back) 95
    The Use of the Prefix 'Pag' with a Verb 97
    Use of the Prefix 'Pagka' When a Verb is Used Indirectly 98
    The Prefix 'Pagka' With an Adjective 98
    Cebuano Expressions: Eskina lang! 99

Words That Seem Hard to Translate 101
    Best – *Pinaka* 101
    Most – *Pinaka* 102
    Say It in Cebuano 103

Chapter 11 105
Bohol: The Land Without A Horse (Kabayo) 106
    Speak Boholano 106

Chapter 12 111

Growing Up in the Islands: Lumad nga Bisaya 112
    Figurative Phrases: English to Cebuano.. 112
    Figurative Phrases: Cebuano to English.. 113
    More Fun With Visayan Tongue Twisters 116

Chapter 13 118
Distinctly Visayan, Distinctly Filipino 119
    Weird Nicknames.. 120
    Words with Repeated Syllables: The Funny Tongue 121
    Double the Words, Double the Fun.. 123

Chapter 14 125
21st Century Visayan Adaptation 126
    Do you have a better translation?... 126
    The Electronic Domain and The Social Media 127

Chapter 16 129
Hashtag in Cebuano, Anyone?... 130
    From #Artless to #Zizz 130

Chapter 17 134
Makagagahum or Gamhanan?.. 135
    Which one are you? 135

Chapter 1

How Much of A Visayan Are You?

Furrowed Brows for The Morrow

What if I say to you?

"Pito ka pitu-pito mipito sa puti nga pato."

In most likelihood, you have already resigned yourself not to read this book since this might be a little too confusing to you now.

This job of learning a new language may seem a cataclysmically confusing immersion into unknown territories but I will walk you through it.

Let's make sense then.

You just got hit by a Visayan tongue 'twister'. (pun intended)

What does it mean?

Before we go deeper into its meaning, let me just remind you of the way Visayan words are enunciated phonetically. /Pi/ in pito is read with a short /i/ sound and not with an /ai/ sound. You can compare it to the sound you hear when reading the English words 'pea' rather than 'pie'. This holds true for other Cebuano or Visayan words with the /i/ vowel; words like: lalaki (male), sinati (to experience), pati (dove). If a Cebuano or Visayan word is meant to have the /ai/ sound, it is spelled with an 'ay': balay (house), sudlay (comb), kilay (eyebrows).

Let's do the translation:
    Pito – seven

    Pitu-pito – tadpole; wriggly little worms of mosquitoes
    Pito – whistle
    Mi pito – whistled (*a verb derived from the root word 'pito'—whistle, by adding the prefix 'mi' which denotes past tense.*)
    Puti – white
    Pato – duck

Thus, the above statement means,

    Seven wriggly little worms whistled at the white duck.

(Don't stress yourself with how the statement lacks sense, rather stress your tongue with pronouncing these words as many times as you can, and as fast as you can. We will get to know more of these in a later chapter in this book.)

Enjoy the alliteration.

    Pito ka pitu-pito mipito sa puti nga pato…pito ka pitu-pito mipito … pito ka pitu-pito … pito!

'In Da Haus' Lingo

    Picture for a second that you are the son or daughter of a cross-cultural marriage. Your mother is Cebuano and your father is of American descent. What do you think will be your spoken language at home? English? Ceb-lish? Cebuano?

    From experience, the former is always the easy choice. When I had my children, everyone around them spoke in English. The nannies, the uncles and aunts, and the other relatives always took the effort to talk in English. English is not so foreign a language to most Filipinos since we have ample exposure to the language in all forms of media. Product packaging and ads are expressed in English. Public documents all bear the standard English format. Instructions on tool or equipment usage are expressed in English. Most anything has an English version to it. You have the option of hearing a mass in Church in English language. The music that is played on the radio is mostly in English. Signs in most establishments are written in English. I know these things are obvious but for those who don't know the culture, it's about time you know that, English might as well be our second language. Our classes in school are mostly carried out with the English language as the medium of instruction.

English is predominantly the more understood language next to Cebuano or the national Filipino language – Tagalog.

So why bother? Why waste your breath on learning the Visayan language when being armed with just English, or Japanese, or Finnish, or German, or French, or Spanish or whatever your mother tongue is, will not stop you from intermingling with the locals for as long as you can understand the most basic English words?

Well, here's why. It's beautiful when you get to interact with the common people in their native tongue. You don't feel so much of a stranger then. This is even more handy if you get to adopt an extended family that hails from Cebu or the neighboring Visayan islands and the rest of the Bisaya-speaking regions including Mindanao, thru marriage or business enterprises or philanthropic or religious pursuits.

It's reassuring to know that you don't call yourself a stranger anymore because you can speak the Cebuano or Visayan language with ease and you have formed in your head a core understanding of how the phrases are crafted or put together.

You do need a handy dictionary to be able to dig up some words and add it to your vocabulary. But rest assured that what you gain here is invaluable in speeding up your mastery of the Cebuano (Visayan) language.

Scenario: (Your child comes to you and tells you the following.)
Mom, I have an activity in school tomorrow.
We are going to celebrate United Nation's Day.
I will be wearing the traditional Filipiniana costume.
I want you and dad to come to witness our talent show.
I will show some of my hidden dance moves.
I'm sure you will be entertained and will be proud of me.

Translation:
Ma, aduna ako'y (I have) aktibidad (an activity) sa eskwelahan (in school) ugma (tomorrow).
Mag-saulog mi (we are going to celebrate) sa adlaw (day) sa United Nations.
Magsuot ko (I will be wearing) ug tradisyonal nga Filipiniana (the traditional Filipiniana) nga sapot (costume).

Gusto nako (I want) *nga ikaw* (that you) *ug si papa* (and dad) *nga mo-adto* (to come) *aron motan-aw* (to witness) *sa among* (our) talent show.

Akong ipakita (I will show) *ang akong mga* (some of my) *tinagu-an nga mga lihok sa pagsayaw* (hidden dance moves).

Sigurado ako (I'm sure) *nga malingaw kamo* (you will be entertained) *ug mahimong mapasigarbohon kanako* (and will be proud of me.)

Full Translation:

Ma, aduna ako'y aktibidad sa eskwelahan ugma.
Magsaulog mi sa adlaw sa United Nations.
Magsuot ko ug tradisyonal nga Filipiniana nga sapot.
Gusto nako nga ikaw ug si Papa moa-adto aron motan-aw sa among talent show.
Akong ipakita ang akong mga tinagu-an nga mga lihok sa pagsayaw.
Sigurado ako nga malingaw kamo ug mahimong mapasigarbohon kanako.

Lessons:

a. Aktibidad is borrowed from the word activity. Alternate word is kalihokan. Root word is 'lihok' for 'act' or 'move'. Kalihokan is movement. But in this context the word aktibidad is more fitting since kalihokan is more apt for a collective movement like a movement in church or public sector or such. Tradisyonal is also a borrowed English word from 'traditional'. In Visayan there are a few words that are adapted from the original English words.

   Droga – Drug
   Empleyado – Employee
   Imbestigasyon – Investigation
   Impormasyon – Information
   Kalibre – Caliber
   Pistola – Pistol
   Positibo – Positive
   Resolusyon – Resolution

b. 'United Nations' and 'talent show' if you noticed, were not translated. Why? It's not practical. It is easier to say those words as is, and they are understood as a generic phrase or term. And this is where functionality of translation is being valued more than being organic in the translation.

But, can we translate these words to pure Visayan? Yes, absolutely. United Nations can be easily said in Cebuano as 'Nagka-hi-usa Nga Mga Kanasuran' (root words: usa/one; nasud/nation.)

Talent Show can be expressed as 'Pasundayag sa Talento' (root word: sundayag/to show; borrowed word: talento/from English word 'talent')

   c. For the most part, the translation is literal, and the clauses can be re-arranged without altering the context. Thus, if you say, "Ma, <u>sa eskwelahan</u> ugma <u>aduna ako'y aktibidad</u>." or "Ma, <u>sa eskwelahan</u> <u>aduna ako'y aktibidad</u> ugma." the same thought is conveyed.

What you have read above is just a simple immersion into the process of translating from English to Cebuano. We will have more examples as we move along.

Not Lost in Translation

Let us pretend that you traveled to Osaka, Japan and you were greeted with, 'Mokarimakka.'

"Are you making a profit?" or 'Mokarimakka' is a traditional greeting in Osaka.

You quite loved the idea of a money-minded and entrepreneurial greeting and wish to say the same thing in Visayan. How will you say it?

So, let's translate in Cebuano,

Are you – ikaw *ba*

Making – naghimo, nihimo
Ug – the (or in this case 'a')
Ginansya – profit (from the English word 'gain')

So, we can fairly transcribe the phrase as,

Ikaw *ba* naghimo ug ginansya?

Note the use of the word **'ba'**,
Ikaw naghimo *ba* ug ginansya?

'Naghimo' can be replaced with another word which bears a similar context as the root word 'himo'. See how the original word and the other words can be used in the above context:

Himo – make
Angkon – acquire
Baton – possess
Mugna – create

Thus,

Ikaw ba nag-angkon ug ginansya?
Ikaw ba nagbaton ug ginansya?
Ikaw ba nagmugna ug ginansya?

But, the more sensible way to express the same thought on the streets of Visayas would be,

Aduna ka ba'y ginansya?

Note the word,
Aduna – have, having

Which translates the last phrase as,
Are you having gains?
Or
Are you having profit?

Lesson:
'Ba' is a word that is used to direct a question.
You are – ikaw

Are you – ikaw *ba*

Change a narrative statement into a query using '**ba**'.

Declarative: Nakahuman ka sa kolehiyo. (You finished college.)
Interrogative: Nakahuman ka **ba** sa kolehiyo. (Did you finish college?)

Going back to the originally translated phrase, 'Mokarimakka', we are simply using it to illustrate the process of decoding a foreign term and converting it to the Visayan equivalent. What better way to do that than to pick a term that is not easily forgotten. In truth though, you will seldom hear other people asking you and being so forthright about your profit or how much money you make unless they are your family.

The more acceptable greeting in Cebuano (Visayan) would be:

'Komusta ang atong negosyo, bay?
'Komusta ang atong negosyo, pre?
'Komusta ang atong panginabuhi, bay?
'Komusta ang atong panginabuhi, pre?

Negosyo – business
Panginabuhi – livelihood
Pre, bay, pare – a colloquial term for brother

Note: Also observe the use of the words 'ato' (ours).

If you think about it, if you are the owner of the business and I am just your neighbor asking about how your business is going, why would I use:

Ato – our

When in fact, it is your business and I have nothing to do with it.

Why not use?

Imo – your

Thus,

Komusta ang imong negosyo, bay?

The answer is, this is a common convention for the sake of being polite. This simmers down the impact of being just another nosy neighbor and transcends the message to that of a genuinely concerned friend.

Komusta ang imong negosyo bay?
(It sounds so exclusive to you so why would you bother sharing information about it?)
Komusta ang atong negosyo bay?
(This gives the aura of 'we are in this together, and feel free to share with me.')

I am pointing this out because you will hear this quite often, and sometimes even in situations where it's literally impossible for someone to share something with you.

Sakit ba gihapon ang atong likod, lola?
(Does our back still hurt, grandma?)

This is an alternate way of asking,

'Does your back still hurt, grandma?' with empathy.

Chapter 2

Say It Like A Cebuano

Before delving into the lessons that you need to assimilate, to get a clear understanding of how to translate English to Cebuano and vice versa, let us quickly learn these phrases and their translations.

The first translation that is provided is the closest literal translation. The second translation is the way the phrase is expressed when spoken, or the way you hear them on the streets on any given day, by the locals.

Conversely, another translation in English is given for the spoken version, to guide you on how the expression came to be.

The common phrases translated to their Cebuano equivalent.

a. I'm afraid if I tell you, I'd have to kill you.
   Literal translation: Mahadlok ko nga kon sultihan ko ikaw, ako usab ikaw nga pagapatyon.
   Spoken Version: *Patyon usa tika, una ka masayud.* (I'll kill you first, before you know.)

b. Tell it to the judge.
   Literal translation: Adto isugid sa huwes.
   Spoken Version: *Kinsa'y imong ilaron?* (Who are you trying to fool?)

c. I can't believe you just did that!
   Literal translation: Di ko katuo nga imong gibuhat na!
   Spoken Version: *Pastilan, wa ko magdahum!* (Could not conceive of it!)

d. Try and try until you succeed.
   Literal translation: Paningkamot gyud hangtud ka molampos.
   Spoken Version: *Antus, aron ma-santos.* (Suffer so you will become a saint.)

e. Give me a break.

Literal translation: Hatagi ko ug panahon nga makapahulay. (Give me time to rest.)

Spoken Version: *Papahuwaya tawon ko ninyo!* (Let me rest.)

f. She is such a witch.
Literal translation: Ang pagka mangtas na lang baya niya!
Spoken Version: *Mangtas gyud!* (Real witch!)

g. When can I ever get a straight answer here?
Literal translation: Kanus-a pa man ko makakuha ug klaro nga tubag diri?
Spoken Version: *Kinsa'y naay tarong nga tubag?* (Who has the right answer?)

h. I can't stand how dumb people are!
Literal translation: Di nako ma-antus ang kabugo sa mga tawo diri!
Spoken Version: *Pagkabogo na lang gyud!* (Absolutely stupid.)

i. I wasn't born yesterday.
Literal translation: Wala ko gipakatawo kagahapon.
Spoken Version: *Nag-una ko sa duyan nimo.* (I was ahead of you in the crib.)

j. Keep it to yourself.
Literal translation: Itago sa imong kaugalingon.
Spoken Version: *Ay, hiloma na lang na!* (Just shush it.)

k. All talk, no action.
Literal translation: Istorya ra, way buhat.
Spoken Version: *Istorya ra'y ga daghan nimo.* (It's all talk that you have so much of.)

l. Good at promises, not at keeping them.
Literal translation: Maayo mo sa-ad, apan dili motuman.
Spoken Version: *Way 'palabra de honor'.* (No 'word of honor'.)

Chapter 3

Get to Know The Basics

This section will re-introduce to you some of the most common words in Cebuano, pre-supposing that you already have a bit of exposure to the language.

Basic Visayan Words That You Need to Understand

Ang – a; the
A dog (*ang* iro)
The cat (*ang* iring)

Aron – to; so that
I came *to* say goodbye. (Mianhi ko *aron* manamilit.)
Get the ball *so that* we can leave. (Kuha-a ang bola *aron* kita makabiya.)

Ba – inquisitive (used in interrogatory statements)
Did you fall? (Nahulog ka ba?)

Diay – really; oh; so; indeed
Indeed, she took the money. (Iya *diay* nga gikuha ang kwarta.)

Gayud – certainly; indeed
That's *certainly* the truth. (Mao *gayud* kana ang kamatuoran.)

Gud – (grammatical filler for emphasis)
This is the most effective (Mao *gud* kini ang pinaka epektibo)

Lagi – certainly; of course
I will do, *certainly*. (Ako nga buhaton *lagi*.)

Lang – just; almost
This is *just* the beginning. (Kini *lang* ang sinugdanan.)

Man – also; too (grammatical filler word)
It is, *also*. (Mao *man*.)

Mao – is
She *is* the one that I saw. (Siya *mao* ang akong nakit-an.)

Mao gyud – is indeed
This man *is indeed* the best doctor in town. (Kining tawhana *mao gayud* ang pinakabatikan nga doctor niining lungsora.)

Na – already
Your husband is *already* here. (Ang imong bana ania *na* diri.)

Nga – which, that is
The gate *which* is painted white (Ang gangha-an *nga* gipintalan ug puti)

O – or
This *or* that? (Kini *o* kana?)

Oy – hey
Hey, no! (Dili *oy*!)
Hey, don't! (Ayaw *oy*!)

Pa – yet
Not *yet*. (Wala *pa*.)

Sa – at, in, on, by, over, of
At the corner *of* (*Sa* eskina *sa*
On the road (*sa* karsada
By the water (*sa* tubig)

Uban – with
Come *with* me. (Kuyog *uban* kanako.)

Ug – and
Ikaw *ug* ako. (You *and* I.)

Examples

The dog **and** the butterfly.
Ang iro **ug** *ang* alibangbang.

The mermaid **at** Punta Engano.
Ang kataw **sa** *Punta Engano.*

Are you going to talk **or** stay quiet?
*Motingog ka **o** mohilom?*

Why are you sad young girl?
*Nganong naguol **man** ka day?*
*Nganong naguol **man** ikaw inday?*

The lies **that** he told you.
*Ang mga bakak **nga** iyang gisulti kanimo.*

Let's dissect these translations:
    Is it **just** that easy?
    *Ingon ana **na lang** ba kasayon?*

    Is it **this** easy?
    *Ingon **ini** ba kasayon?*

Ingon ana – Like that
Ingon ini – Like this
Root word: Maingon - Like/similar/same/comparable
Ana – That (shortened form of 'kana')
    (Root word: Kana – That)
Ini – This (shortened form of 'kini')
    (Root word: Kini – This)

Full phrases:
Maingon kini ana (This like that)
Maingon kana ini (That like this)
Lang – Just (used here to mean simply)

Kasayon – That Easy
(Root word : Sayon/Easy)

Ingon ini ba **di-ay** kalisud?
Is it **really** this hard?

Ingon ani **man gyud di-ay** kalisud.
It is **really** this hard.

When *ini* and *ana* is being used, imagine holding a piece of something in both hands against another person holding something in both hands opposite you.

When you say 'ini', 'kini' think exactly about what you are holding in your hands,

Likewise, when you say 'ana', 'kana' imagine pointing your finger at one of the objects that the other person is holding.

Ini, ana, kini, kana does not necessarily imply tangible objects. *Ini* could be used to refer to someone's state of emotions or a situation and likewise with the word 'ana'.

Let's examine the following translations:

The things he told me about you are **really** true.
Ang iyang gipangsulti kanako bahin kanimo, <u>tinu-od gayud</u>.
Ang iyang gipangsulti kanako mahitungod kanimo, tinu-od gayud.

Rearranging the clauses:
<u>Tinuod</u> **gayud** *ang iyang gipangsulti kanako* **bahin** *kanimo.*
<u>Tinuod</u> **gayud** *ang iyang gipangsulti kanako* **mahitungod** *kanimo.*

Tinu-od – True
Tinu-od gayud – Really true
Root word: Sulti (tell)
Gisulti - Told
Gipangsulti – Things that are told
Gipangsulti kanako – Things that are told to me
Bahin kanimo – **About** you

Alternate:
Mahitungod kanimo – **About** you

So, what if we say instead the phrases below? Will it alter the meaning of the statement above?

Ang iyang gipangsulti kanako bahin kanimo, tinuod **gyud di-ay**.
Ang iyang gipangsulti kanako bahin kanimo, tinuod **man gyud di-ay**.
The answer is NO. These statements bear the same meaning but with a more emphatic tone to it.

Now let's try modifying the statement above.

The things he told me about you are **not true**.
Ang iyang gipangsulti kanako bahin kanimo, **dili tinuod**.
Ang iyang gipangsulti kanako bahin kanimo, dili diay tinu-od.
Ang iyang gipangsulti kanako bahin kanimo, dili man gyud tinu-od.
Ang iyang gipangsulti kanako bahin kanimo, dili man gyud diay tinu-od.

Dili tinuod –**Not** true

Negation

Lesson on Negation:

The word 'dili'(not) can be easily added to express the opposite meaning of a word or a phrase.

Colorful – Mabulukon
Color*less* – *Dili* Mabulukon

Believable – Katuho-an
*Un*believable – *Dili* Katuho-an

Will travel – Mobiyahe
Will *not* travel – *Dili* Mobiyahe

Patient –Pasensyoso
*Im*patient – *Dili* Pasensyoso

Just – Makatoronganon
Unjust – *Di*li makatoronganon

Lesson on Negation:

The word 'wala' (none) can be added to a phrase to express a negative or the opposite meaning.

Nasayud – Know
Wala nasayud – Does *not* know

Nahinayon – pushed through
Wala mahinayon – did *not* push through

Nakatulog – has slept
Wala nakatulog – has *not* slept

Other words:

Wala'y dungog – *dis*honorable (root word: dungog/honor)
Wala'y uwaw – shame*less* (root word: shame/uwaw)
Way batasan – crude; *un*refined; vulgar (root word: batasan/character)
Way buot – *ir*responsible; childish (root word: panimu-ot/consciousness)
Way kalipay – resentful; *un*happy (root word: kalipay/happiness)
Way kukalu-oy – in a merci*less* manner (root word: kalu-oy/mercy)
Way kwarta – poor; *no* money (root word: kwarta/money)
Way sapot – naked; *no* clothing (root word: sapot/clothing)
Way siguro – uncertain (root word: siguro/sure)
Way silingan – *un*friendly; indifferent (root word: silingan/neighbor)
Way ugma – *no* future (root word: kaugma-on/future)

Most of these words can be transformed to its opposite connotation by replacing 'wala' or 'wala'y' or 'way' with the word:

Naa or naa'y or na-ay

Some of the above words take a different form when transformed:

Way siguro – uncertain (adj)

Sigurado – certain (adj)

Way buot – *ir*responsible (adj)
Buotan – good natured; one who is mature in his ways (adj)

Way kukalu-oy – in a merci*less* manner (adv)
Maluy-anon – in a merciful way (adv)

Basic Sentence Construction

A declarative statement typically begins with the word 'ang' (a or the) to refer to a noun or an event in a subject clause. It is then followed by the predicate composed of an action word or other set of words to complete the thought in a sentence.

It is as simple as subject(S) plus predicate(P).

Ang among bisita natulog sa banig.
Our visitor slept on the mat.
    S: Ang among bisita
    P: natulog sa banig

Ang akong bisita miinom ug tuba.
My visitor drank coconut wine.
    S: Ang akong bisita
    P: mi-inom ug tuba

Ang imong bisita mikatkat sa puno-an sa lubi.
Your visitor climbed up the coconut tree.
    S: Ang imong bisita
    P: mikatkat sa puno-an sa lubi

Ang inyong bisita kahibalo mosulti ug maayong gabii.
Your visitor knows how to say good evening.
    S: Ang inyong bisita
    P: kahibalo mosulti ug maayong gabii

Ang iyang bisita dili pili-an sa pagkaon.
His/Her visitor is not picky with food.
    S: Ang iyang bisita
    P: dili pili-an sa pagkaon

Ang akong bisita maka-kunsumisyon.
My visitor is a pain in the bum.
    S: Ang akong bisita
    P: maka-kunsumisyon

Ang atong bisita halangdon.
Our visitor is honorable.
    S: Ang atong bisita
    P: halangdon

Ang bata natulog.
The child is sleeping.
    S: Ang bata
    P: natulog

Ang bata miinom ug tubig.
The child drank water.
    S: Ang bata
    P: mi-inom ug tubig

Ang bata mikatkat sa punoan sa kahoy.
The child climbed up the tree.
    S: Ang bata
    P: mikatkat sa punoan sa kahoy

Ang bata kahibalo na mosulti.
The child already knows how to talk.
    S: Ang bata
    P: kahibalo na mosulti

Ang bata pili-an sa pagkaon.
The child is very picky with food.
    S: Ang bata
    P: Pili-an kaayo sa pagkaon

Ang bata badlungon.
The child is mischievous.
    S: Ang bata
    P: badlungon

Rearranging Phrases

Natulog sa banig ang among bisita.
Natulog ang among bisita sa banig.

The rule is to complete a thought, so the statement makes sense.

What: Natulog (slept)
Where: Sa banig (on the mat)
Who: Ang bisita (the visitor)
Whose: Amo (ours)

Miinom ug tuba ang akong bisita.
Miinom ang akong bisita ug tuba.
What: miinom
What: ug tuba
Who: ang bisita
Whose: ako-a

Mikat-kat sa puno-an sa lubi ang imong bisita.
Mikat-kat ang imong bisita sa puno-an sa lubi.
What: mikat-kat
Where: sa puno-an
What kind: sa lubi
Who: ang bisita
Whose: imo

Kahibalo mosulti ug maayong gabii ang inyong bisita.
Kahibalo ang inyong bisita mosulti ug maayong gabii.
What: kahibalo mosulti
What: maayong gabii
Who: ang bisita
Whose: inyo-a

Dili pili-an sa pagkaon ang iyang bisita.
Dili pili-an ang iyang bisita sa pagkaon.

What: dili pili-an
What: sa pagkaon
Who: ang bisita
Whose: iya-a

Halangdon ang atong bisita.
What: halangdon
Who: ang bisita
Whose: ato-a

Let's learn to dissect phrases using this example.

There is a good reason to feel like you are contributing to a worthy cause by going halfway across the world to help feed hungry children.

Adunay maayo nga rason – there is a good reason
Aron mobati nga ikaw sama sa nagadugang – to feel like you are contributing
Sa mapuslanon nga katuyo-an – to a worthy cause
Pinaagi sa pag adto – by going
Sa layo nga bahin sa kalibutan – halfway across the world
Aron motabang ug paka-on – to help feed
Sa mga nagutman nga kabataan – hungry children

Let's rearrange phrases:

How: Pinaagi sa pag adto
Where: sa layo nga bahin sa kalibutan
What: aron motabang ug paka-on
Who: sa mga nagutman nga kabataan
What: adunay maayo nga rason
What: aron mobati nga ikaw sama sa nagadugang
What: sa mapuslanon nga katuyo-an

By going halfway across the world to help feed hungry children, there is a good reason to feel like you are contributing to a worthy cause.

Let's rephrase some more.

Aron motabang ug paka-on
sa mga nagutman nga kabataan
pina-agi sa pag adto
sa layo nga bahin sa kalibutan
adunay maayo nga rason
aron mobati nga ikaw sama sa nagadugang
sa mapuslanon nga katuyo-an

To help feed hungry children, by going halfway across the world, there is a good reason to feel like you are contributing to a worthy cause.

Now you translate this on your own:

There is a good reason to feel like you are contributing to a worthy cause to help feed hungry children by going halfway across the world.

Was the context of this statement altered by rearranging the phrases?

The Plural Form

When you hear the word 'mga' always remember plural form.

Panghitabo – event
Mga panghitabo – events

Tawo – a person
Mga tawo – people

Vehicle – sakyanan
Vehicles – *Mga* sakyanan

Reason – Rason
Mga Rason – Reasons

Some words can also be pluralized by adding the 'es' or 's' to the word. This is typical for words with a foreign origin.

Okasyon – mga okasyon, okasyones (/o/-/kas/-/yo/-/nes/)
Obligasyon – mga obligasyon, obligasyones (/ob/-/li/-/gas/-/yo/-/nes/)
Bendisyon – mga bendisyon, bendisyones (/ben/-/dis/-/yo/-/nes/)
Manzana – mga manzana, manzanas (/man/-/za/-/na/)
Cucharita – mga kutsarita, cucharitas (/cu/-/cha/-/ri/-/tas/)

The Root of Words

Perhaps the best way to translate words in one language to another language is to decipher the meaning based on the root word and its context when combined with other words.

Can you decode the following phrases?

Cebuano to English

1. Katapusang singgit
    Singgit – scream
    Tapos – end
    Katapusan - ?

2. Kasinati-an sa kinabuhi
    Kinabuhi – Life
    Sinati – To relish in existence
    Kasinati-an - ?

3. Ka-ugma-on sa mga anak
    Mga anak – Children
    Ugma – Tomorrow
    Kaugma-on - ?

4. Bililhon nga mga pulong
    Mga pulong – Words
    Bili – Worth
    Bilil-hon - ?

5. Kalibutanong panginahanglan
    Panginahanglan – need
    Kalibutan – earth
    Kalibutanon - ?

6. Madag-umon nga mga langit
    Langit – sky

Dag-um – dark
Madag-umon - ?

Here are the translated phrases:

1. *The last* scream
2. *Experience* in life
3. The *future* of the children
4. *Precious* words
5. *Worldly* desires
6. *Gloomy* skies

English to Cebuano

1. Extreme brevity
    Brief – short (mubo)
    Brevity – shortness (ka mubo)
    Extreme – Tuman

    Tuman nga ka-mubo

2. A spirited debate
    Debate – Panaglantugi
    Spirited – of high spirits, of high energy, heated
        -   Mainiton (Root word: heat/init)

    Mainitong panaglantugi

3. Lilliputian world

    World – Kalibutan
    Lilliput in nature – miniature, very small in size
    (Small: Gamay)
    (Smaller than small: Gamatoy)

    Gamatoy nga kalibutan

4. Power of persuasion

> Persuasion – the act of persuading (Pag-agni)
> Persuade – agni
> Power – gahum

Gahum sa pag-agni

5. Audible laughter

> Laughter – katawa
> Audible – Root word: audio/sound
> Sound (tingog)
> Audible – can be heard
> Hear – dungog
> Root word ear: dunggan
> Audible: madungog

Madungog nga katawa

Chapter 4

Conjunctions And More

rm yourself with a good understanding of the most common conjunctions. Conjunctions connect two or more clauses in a sentence be it a *declarative* or an *interrogative* statement.

After – Human sa
There is a rise of airborne diseases **after** the winter months.
Adunay pag-umento sa sakit nga makatakod pinaagi sa hangin **human sa** mga matugnaw nga mga buwan.

Albeit – Bisan pa
The students did as they were instructed, **albeit** they were unhappy.
Ang mga estudyante mihimo sumala sa pagmando, **bisan pa** kon dili sila malipayon.

Although – Bisan pa
The driver insisted on taking a different route, **although** I have already told him that I don't mind the heavy flow of the traffic.
Ang drayber mi-insister sa pag latas ug lahi nga rota, **bisan pa** nga ako na siya nga na-sultihan nga wala koy problema sa bug-at nga daloy sa trapiko.

And – Ug
I am an engineer by day **and** a writer by night.
Usa ako ka enhinyero sa adlaw **ug** usa ka manunulat sa gabii.

Because – Tungod kay, tungod sa
I will cut on spending and save every penny **because** I want to buy a brand-new luxury car.
Akong putlon ang pagpunay ug palit ug akong tigumon ang matag sinsilyo **tungod kay** gusto ko mopalit ug bag-o nga maluho nga sakyanan.

Before – Sa dili pa
We have to say a prayer of thanksgiving **before** we partake on this day's meal.

Mag-ampo kita sa pasalamat **sa dili pa** *kita mo-ambit sa grasya niining adlawa.*

But – Pero, Apan
I would need your help **but** not this soon.
Kinahanglanon nako ang imong tabang **apan** *dili ingon ani kasayo.*

Considerably – Sa pag-ila
Considerably, I am shocked to hear that you have been fired, knowing that you spearheaded the most profitable achievememts in this company.

Sa pag-ila, *ako nahikurat nga nakadungog nga ikaw na-taktak sa trabaho, ubos sa kasayuran nga imo nga gipanguluhan ang mga pinaka mabungahon nga mga nakab-ot niining kompanya.*

e.g. (for example) – Sama sa, Susama sa
I don't like it when you disrespect me, **e.g.**, when you start walking away while I'm still talking to you.

Dili nako gusto kung di ka motahod nako, **susama sa**, *kung mobiya ka bisan kung ako nakigsulti pa kanimo.*

Either Or – Kini o Kana
Either you surrender in peace **or** I'll be forced to shoot you.
Kining mohural ka sa kalinaw **o** *kanang mapugos ako nga pusilon ka.*

Etc. (and others) – Ug uban pa
My children want to go to the store to get school supplies like pen, paper, crayons, **etc.**

Even if – Bisan kon
The mayor attended the rally **even if** he was told to avoid public appearances due to a severe threat.

Ang mayor mi-atender sa panagtapok **bisan kon** *gi-awhag siya nga likayan ang pagpakita sa publiko tungod sa seryoso nga hulga.*

Even though – Bisan nga

She came in at the office on a Monday, **even though** she knows that the office is closed.

Mi-adto siya sa opisina sa Lunes, **bisan nga** naka hibawo siya nga ang opisina serado.

First and Foremost – Una sa tanan
You need to straighten your act, **first and foremost**.

Angay nimong tul-iron ang imong pama-agi, **una sa tanan**.

For – Para, Alang
We need to educate our children **for** the welfare of our nation.

Angay nato nga edukahon ang atong mga anak **alang** sa kaugma-on sa atong nasud.

Former – Nahiuna
I wanted to travel the world. I also want to jump on a plane. But I think the **former** is the more adventurous pursuit.

Gusto ko nga mosuroy sa kalibutan. Gusto usab ko nga mo-ambak gikan sa eroplano. Pero sa akong pagtuo ang **nahi-una** mas mahinamon nga pamagdoy.

i.e. (that is) – Mao nga
I am not going to tolerate your crazy antics anymore, **that is**, next time when you say we're done, we're done.

Dili ko na agwantahon ang imong mga kabuang, **mao nga**, sa sunod kung moingon ka nga wala na kita, wala na kita.

If – Kung
You get a five percent discount **if** you do your shopping on a Tuesday.

Makakuha ka ug singko por syento nga hangyo **kung** mangompra ka inig ka Martes.

In as much as – Sa gika-ingon nga
In as much as the mother didn't want her son to spend so much time with his friends, she didn't want him to feel left out.

Sa gikaingon nga ang iyang inahan dili gusto nga ang iyang anak nga magpunay ug yampungad uban sa iyang mga higala, dili usab niya gusto nga ang iyang anak mobati nga siya nasalikway.

Indeed – Gyud, Mao gyud, man
Having a warm cup of coffee is **indeed** a nice addition to an already great morning.

Ang pag-inom ug mainit nga kape **mao gyud** ang nindot nga dugang sa nindot na daan nga kabuntagon.

Instead

Latter – Na-uwahi

Trust a few. Row your own canoe. And when you think of it, the **latter** is the more important test of courage.

Salig sa pipila lamang. Bugsayi ang imong kaugalingong baruto. Ug kon imo kining pamalandungan, ang **na-uwahi** mao ang mas importante nga pagsukod sa imong kaisog.

Likewise – Ug susama usab niini

To treat others with kindness is a praiseworthy attitude. **Likewise**, to treat yourself with kindness is a praiseworthy endeavor.

Ang pagtratar sa uban sa kaayo usa ka dalaygon nga kinaiya. **Ug susama usab niini**, ang pagtratar sa imong kaugalingon sa kaayo usa ka dalaygon nga katuyo-an.

Neither Nor – Nungka/Ni

Neither your rejection **nor** your criticism will discourage me from pursuing my dreams.

Nungka ang inyong pagsalikway **ni** ang inyong pagsaway makahunong kanako sa akong pagkab-ot sa akong mga damgo.

Or – O

You can leave **or** you can stay.

Makabiya ka **o** magpabilin.

Otherwise – Kay kon dili

Do as you're told **otherwise**, you will be charged with insubordination.

Tumana ang gisugo kanimo **kay kon dili** mapasangilan ka sa pagka dili matinumanon.

Since – Tungod lagi kay, Tungod kay

The teacher gave her an excellent mark **since** she passed all graded exams with flying colors.

Ang magtutudlo mihatag kaniya ug pinakataas nga marka **tungod kay** mabulukon niyang gipasar ang tanang gipang-graduhan nga pasulit.

So – Busa

I didn't get the job **so** I started my own business.

Wala nako makuha ang trabaho **busa** nagsugod ko sa akong negosyo.

Therefore - Entonses

Frogs love the rain, **therefore,** *they started singing when it rained hard.*
Ang mga baki gusto sa uwan, **entonses,** *nagsugod sila ug panganta sa dihang mikusog ug uwan.*

Thus – Mao nga

You have a great potential on your career, **thus,** *I'm encouraging you to persist and finish your degree.*
Aduna kay maayong purohan sa imong karera, **mao nga,** *ako nag-awhag kanimo nga mopadayon ug tapuson ang imong kurso.*

While – Samtang

She was praying the rosary, **while** *he was driving on the highway.*
Nag-rosaryo siya **samtang** *nagmaneho siya sa halapad ug delikado nga dalan.*

Yet – Apan

She said that she is rich, **yet** *she is scraping for the last penny that she could save.*
Mi-ingon siya nga datu siya **apan** *iyang gidaginot ang pinaka sinsilyo nga iyang mahipos.*

Conventions You Need to Know And Learn

If you have been to Cebu and the neighboring islands for a while now, you can tell the difference between a Cebuano speaker from other Visayans using this convention:

The Shortened Form of Words (Cebuano vs Visayan)

In Cebuano words are usually shortened compared to the typical Visayan word thus,

House
    Balay (Visayan)
    Bay (Cebuano)

Inside
    Sulod (Visayan)
    Sud (Cebuano)

Fell
    Nahulog (Visayan)
    Nahug (Cebuano)

Fire
    Kalayo (Visayan)
    Kayo (Cebuano)

Sleep
    Katulog (Visayan)

Katug (Cebuano)

Just
    Lamang (Visayan)
    Lang (Cebuano)

Cebuano with 'w' instead of the Visayan 'l'

No shame
    Walay ulaw (Visayan)
    Way uwaw (Cebuano)

Flower
    Bulak (Visayan)
    Buwak (Cebuano)

Was late
    Na-ulahi (Visayan)
    Na-uwahi (Cebuano)

Same Word, Different Meanings

Some words have two different meanings as well. The diction and stressing of the syllable when spoken helps differentiate the meanings.

Sala
    Sin (noun)
    Living room (noun)

Buwan
    Month (noun)
    Moon (noun)

Baga
Thick (adjective)
Glowing ember (noun)

If you are just learning to understand the Cebuano (Visayan) language, perhaps a good exposure to the variances in how the language is crafted is to visit different places and listen attentively to the phrases that are thrown into the open. Mingling with the locals will allow you a better chance of digesting the conversational patterns including the diction of the words and phrases.

Chapter 5

Speak Up: English to Cebuano

50 Phrases You Need to Master

1. Good for you!
    Maayo nimo da!

2. Absolutely
    Siyempre
    Oo

3. In the meantime
    Sa pagka karon
    Sa kasamtangan

4. Can't say for sure
    Di ko makaingon nga siguro
    Di ko maka siguro
    Di nako masiguro

5. I don't know
    Wa ko kahibalo
    Wa ko kabawo
    Wa ko masayud
    Ambot

6. Oh really?
    O mao ba?
    Tinuod ba?
    Tinuod ka diha?
    Saba ka, diha? (Shut up, really?)

7. Get out of here!
    Diha, mao ba?

      Hilom ka! Mao ba?
      Di katuho-an! (Unbelievable)

8. Shut up!
      Paghilom!
      Ayaw'g langas!
      Ayaw'g saba!
      Saba na! (Shush already!)

9. You're making me uncomfortable.
      Imo kong gipabati ug kabalaka.
      Mora'g dili na ni maayo da! (This is not looking good right now.)

10. Let's agree on ...
      Magsabot ta nga ...
      Magsinabtanay ta nga ...
      Diyl? (Borrowed word for 'deal')

11. I can't believe you did it!
      Di ko katuo nga imo nang gibuhat!
      Di ko katuo!
      Sus, maryosep! (biblical and perhaps to some may be offensive)
      Sus!

12. Congratulations!
      Congratz!
      Dalaygon! (Worthy of praise)
      Mainitong pagdayeg! (Warm words of praise)
      Malipayong pagsaulog! (Happy celebration)

13. Thank you Lord!
      Salamat Ginoo ko!
      Salamat Dios ko!

14. I'm not in the mood for this.
      Wa ko sa gana ini karon.
      Ayaw ko ug samoka. (Don't bother me.)

15. Oh well
      A, basta
      Aw mao na

16. May karma catch up on you.
    Gaba-an pa unta ka.
    Ang gaba di magsaba. (Karma will befall you quietly.)

17. You are so lucky.
    Swerte kaayo ka.
    Bulahan kaay' ka.
    Swerte nimo oy!
    Swerteha da!

18. Please stop.
    Undangi palihug.
    Palihug ug hunong.
    Hunong na intawon.
    Sakto na.

19. You're so annoying.
    Makapungot kaayo ka.
    Gisapot ko nimo. (I'm in a bad mood because of you.)

20. I don't get it.
    Wa ko kasabot.
    Di ko ka tuo. (I can't believe it.)
    Wa ko ka-jee! (Colloquial 'jee' for the sound of letter G for the word 'get')

21. I am floored!
    Nakalitan ako. (I am shocked.)
    Nahipugwat ako. (I am dumbfounded.)
    Way kabutangan sa akong kalipay. (I'm so ecstatic, nowhere to put my happiness)
    Di ko katu-o! (This is beyond belief.)

22. That's amazing!
    Pagka-anindot gyud ana!
    Pagka-maayo na lang gyud!
    Pagkanindot oi!
    Nindota ah!

23. I'll deal with you later.
    Atimanon ra ka nako unya.

Unya ka lang!
Katilaw gyud ka ba! (You'll have a dose of ...)
Huwat ka lang. (Just wait for it.)
Bantay ka lang. (Watch out.)

24. You are so rude.
    Bastos kaayo ka ba.
    Pintas gyud kaayo ka.
    Salbahis lagi ka.
    Bastos! (Unrefined, ill-mannered, no etiquette.)

25. Please behave yourself.
    Pagtarong mo sa inyong kaugalingon.
    Pagtarong ra gud mo.

26. This better be good.
    Unta maayo ni ha.
    Hinaut nga dili ko magmahay. (Hope I won't regret this.)
    Salig, ayaw'g laum. ('Trust but don't hope' expressed with sarcasm.)

27. I don't trust you.
    Wa koy salig nimo.

28. I have an uneasy feeling about this.
    Lain akong paminaw ani da.
    Mora'g delikado man ni. (This seems dangerous.)
    Ga duha-duha ko ini. (I'm in doubt about this.)

29. Oh wow, this is a piece of paradise.
    Oy kanindot, mao ra man ni ug Paraiso.
    Mora ug Paraiso da!
    Pagka-anindot na lang ba gyud oi!

30. I can't stop my emotions.
    Di nako mapugngan ang akong gibati.

31. Sorry, I'm getting a little too emotional.
    Pasensya, nadala ko sa akong pagbati. (I got carried away by my emotions.)

32. Oh, I am the happiest man in the world!

Ay, ako ang pinakamalipayon nga binuhat sa kalibutan!

33. I hate you!
    Ako kang gikasilagan!
    Nasilag ako kanimo!
    Layas! (Pack your stuff and leave!)

34. Thank you so much.
    Salamat kaayo.
    Daghang salamat. (Many thanks.)

35. My pleasure.
    Akong gikalipay.

36. You're welcome.
    Walay sapayan.
    Way sapayan.
    Basta ikaw. (If it's you, anytime.)

37. I love you above all things.
    Gihigugma ko ikaw labaw sa tanang butang.
    Gihigugma ko ikaw labaw sa tanan.

38. This is getting serious.
    Mao ra ug seryoso na man ni.
    Di na gyud ni komedya. (This is not a joke no more.)
    Di na gyud ni duwa-duwa. (This is not a game anymore.)
    Tini-nuod na gyud. (All for real.)

39. This is such a bad idea.
    Dili ni maayo nga ideya da.

40. You are ridiculous.
    Pagka wala gyud nimo'y kwenta. (You absolutely make no sense, whatsoever.)

41. Please leave me alone.
    Palihug biya-i ko.
    Gusto ko nga mag-inusa ra. (I want to be alone.)

42. I don't want to talk right now.

Dili ko gusto makigsulti kang bisan kinsa karon.
Gusto ko nga maghilom. (I want to be quiet.)

43. I have nothing to say.
    Wala koy ika-sulti.
    Wala koy matug-an kaninyo. (Nothing I can divulge or share to you.)

44. I have no prior knowledge.
    Wa ko kahibawo daan.
    Wa koy daan nga kasayuran.
    Wa gyud ko nasayud.

45. I am totally unaware.
    Wa gyud ko kabantay.
    Wa gyud ko kahibawo bisan dyutay lang.
    Wa ko'y kalibutan.
    'No earth' gyud ko.

(This is one of my favorite things to say when I want to mean I don't know. 'No earth' is a literal translation of the phrase 'way kalibutan' in English.

Kalibutan – Earth
Wala – No, None
Wa'y – Concatenated form of 'wala ay'
Ay – is just a filler word so the phrase doesn't sound incompletely awkward.

Thus,
Wala ay kalibutan or wa'y kalibutan or 'no earth'

But how did this phrase come about? What's the relevance to awareness or knowledge? 'Kalibutan' as used in 'way kalibutan' does not mean **earth**, rather, kalibutan in this context means a perceptive knowledge of things around you or your awareness, simply put. Thus, this phrase or expression is a twisted play of words, but it is meant as a funny way of saying, "I'm totally in the dark of things!")

46. Can you forgive me?
    Pasaylo-a ako.
    Pwede ko nimo pasaylo-on?

47. Can you give me another chance?
    Palihug hatagi ako ug laing higayon.

Pwede ba ko nimo hatagan ug usa pa ka tsansa. (Can you give me one more chance.)

48. Can you spare some consideration for me?
Pwede ba ako nimo hatagan ug konsiderasyon?
Pwede ba ako nimo sabton? (Spare me some understanding.)
Sabta ko. (Try to understand me.)

49. Can you listen to me for a bit?
Paminawa ra gud ko kadyot.
Paminaw ba.

50. Tell me about it.
Suginli ko bahin ini.
Istoryahi!

Chapter 6

Translation 101

Framing the Subject

f you want to understand the language with a more literary intent, that is, you want to be a masterful writer of the Cebuano (Visayan) language then you have to understand the basic requirement of a sentence structure.

Similar to the English language which dwells on subject and predicate agreement, the Cebuano lingo also adheres to the same format.

The subject part can be introduced by answering questions like what or who or where or or when or why or how or how many. Examine closely the illustration that follow.

>   What, unsa
>   Who, kinsa
>   Where, asa
>   When, kanus-a
>   Why, ngano
>   How, unsa-on (or in what way, gi-unsa)
>   How many, pila ka buok

Let's explore:
The answer to the what aspect usually starts with 'ang' (the)
>   Ang bola (the ball)
>   Ang ligid sa sakyanan (the wheel of the car)
>   Ang sakyanan (the vehicle)
>   Ang tawo (the man)
>   Ang bulak (the flower)

The answer to the who aspect usually begins with 'si' (a pointer to refer to a name)
Si Maria (Mary)
Si Juan (John)
Si Presidente Duterte (President Duterte)
Si Dr. Jose Rizal (Dr. Jose Rizal)
Si mama (My mom)
Si lolo (My grandfather)

Pronouns like the ones listed below can also be used to answer the 'who' question
Siya (He/She)
Sila (They)
Ila (Theirs)
Iya (His/hers)

The 'where' part can be answered by 'didto sa' (a pointer to a place similar to saying 'over there').
Didto sa ilawom sa kahoy (Under the tree)
Didto sa likod sa eskwelahan (At the back of the school)
Didto sa ilawom sa dagat (Underneath the sea)
Didto sa tunga sa merkado (in the middle of the market)
Didto sa kanhi natong gipuy-an (the place where we used to live)
Didto sa tumoy sa kalibutan (at the ends of the earth)

Sometimes the word 'didto' can be omitted such that 'sa' will suffice as a replacement for 'didto sa'.
Sa ibabaw sa lamesa (on top of the table)
Sa gawas sa balay (outside the house)
Sa karaang simbahan (at the old church)
Sa tunga sa karsada (in the middle of the road)
Sa taliwala sa kagubot (in the midst of chaos)
Sa unahan sa tulay (further down after the bridge)
Sa among balay (at our house)
Sa balay (at the house)

To construct the where part in an interrogative format the following words are used.
Dis-a
    Dis-a ka gikan? (Where are you from?)
Diin
    Diin ka nagpuyo? (Where do you live?)
Asa

Asa ang imong sakyanan? (Where is your car?)

The answer to these questions can begin with the following words.
- Didto sa (There at)
- Naa sa (Right at)
- Tu-a sa (Over at)

When can be answered by any time-related context. A few words that are time-bound are as follows. Also check the examples that follow.
- Ugma sa (tomorrow by)
- Unya (later)
- Inig ka (by a certain time or period)
- Sa sunod (at the next)
- Kung (means 'when a certain condition is satisfied')

Examples:
- Ugma sa gabii (tomorrow night)
- Ugma sa kaadlawon (tomorrow at dawn)
- Ugma sa udto (tomorrow at noon)
- Unyang hapon (later this afternoon)
- Unyang tingpama-uli (later at dismissal)
- Unya sa panihapon (later at dinnertime)
- Inig ka alas sais sa buntag (by 6 AM)
- Inig ka ugma (by tomorrow)
- Inig katulog (by sleeptime)
- Inig kahuman (by the time it's done)
- Sa sunod nga adlaw (by the following day)
- Sa sunod semana (by next week)
- Sa sunod nga pagsugod sa klase (by the next start of school)
- Kung mosinggit na ako (when I yell)
- Kung mapawong na ang kayo (when the flame is exhausted)
- Kung moabot na ka sa Cebu (when you arrive in Cebu)
- Kung makuha na nimo ang imong bagahe (when you are able to get your luggage)

Why is answered with any declarative statement that conveys reasoning or justification.

The following words are typically used to complete the thought.
- Mao nga (that's why)

Busa (thus)
Kay (because)

Examples:
Naguol man siya busa (She was saddened thus)
Nahiubos ko nimo mao nga (I was upset about you that's why)
Naghimo ka ug istorya mao nga (you made a story that's why)
Gihadlok ko sa akong kaaway busa (I was threatened by my nemesis thus)
Gihunong ang salida kay (the show was stopped because)
Gisumbong ta ka kay (I ratted on you because)
Niingon ka nga ako lang busa (you said that I was the only one thus)
Ni-uli ka nga hubog mao nga (you came home drunk that's why)
Magkuha mi ug...kay (We will get the... because)

The words 'busa', 'mao nga', 'kay' can be used interchangeably.

The 'how' can be answered by 'gi' followed by the root verb word.
Gi-laparo (was smacked)
Gi-laparo sa tuo nga kamot (was slapped by the left hand)
Gi-hagkan (was kissed)
Gi-hagkan sa aping (kissed on the cheek)
Gi-sugat (was welcomed)
Gi-sugat sa palakpakan (welcomed by applause)
Gi-sugat sa makabungog nga palakpakan (welcomed by a thunderous applause)
Gi-sagol (was mixed)
Gi-sagol sa ilimnon (was mixed in the drink)
Gi-sagol sa ilimnon nga makahubog (was mixed in the alcoholic drink)

The 'how many' is always answered by a number, a numerical reference or a collective pronoun.
Lima ka libo ang mitambong (Five thousand attended)
Lima ka libo ka mga tawo ang mitambong (Five thousand people attended)
Duha ka estudyante ang (two students were)
Tanang tawo ang (all the people were)
Tanan ang (Everyone was)
Duha ka dosena sa (two dozen of)
Dyutay ra ang (Only a few)
Usa ug tunga ka kilo nga (one and a half kilo of)

El Niño Mi-sutoy!

Now you might be wondering what's the meaning of the phrase above. We all love the wit of a funny phrase. Right? Let's translate.

El niño – the boy (Spanish)
Mi-sutoy – dashed off (Cebuano)

Thus, what I am trying to convey is,

The boy ran fast.

The only problem is, this is a made-up phrase of Cebuano and Spanish words meant to have a wit about it since 'mi' is also a valid Spanish word which means 'my'.
Mi corazon – my heart
Mi caza – my house

Anyway, 'misutoy' is the past participle form of a real Cebuano action word.

Sutoy – dash off

Thus,

Mi-sutoy – dashed off

Now you have a good way to remember that 'mi' action words belong in the past.

Ang batang lalaki misutoy.
The boy dashed off.

Ang batang lalaki midagan ug kusog.
The boy ran fast.

The Verb Tenses

To complete a sentence, a subject and a predicate is needed. We have tackled the subject part earlier. In this section we will take a plunge on how to construct and deconstruct a verb from Cebuano to Visayan and vice versa.

The predicate in typical fashion holds the action part to complete a thought. And when it comes to action, the format is changed according to time or occurrence – past, present, future, past progressive, present progressive and future progressive, etc.

Say the verb, write:

Past – wrote
Present – write
Future – will write
Past progressive – was writing
Present progressive – is writing
Future progressive – will be writing
Past participle – has written
Present participle – is written
Future participle – will be written

Let's get literal:
    Write – sulat/suwat

Past:
    She wrote on paper.
    Ni – sulat siya sa papel.

Present:
    She writes on paper.
    Nag – sulat siya sa papel.

Future:
    She will write on paper.
    Mo – sulat siya sa papel.

Past progressive:
    She was writing on paper.

Ning-sulat siya sa papel.

Present progressive:
She is writing on paper.
Naga-sulat siya sa papel.

Future progressive:
She will be writing on paper.
Maga-sulat siya sa papel.

Past participle:
She has written on the paper.
Naka-sulat siya sa papel.

Present participle:
Her name is written on the paper.
Ang iyang ngalan nahi-sulat sa papel.

Future participle:
Her name will be written on the paper.
Ang iyang ngalan mahi-sulat sa papel.

In spoken Cebuano, there is no obvious distinction of the progressive and the participle verb formats. The only notable rule is this:

Mo, Mag, Makig, Mang, Ma or the 'M' starting verbs are for future verbs.
Note: Mi verbs is an exception to this M prefix. Mi verbs always denote a past event.

Ni, Nag, Nakig, Nang, Na or the 'N' starting verbs are for past actions.

So how is the present tense denoted in verb format?
Nag, *Nagka*, *Naga* or *Nag*(sige) are the commonly used prefixes.

Present time descriptors are also used to help complete the thought with clarity like:
Kasamtangan – at the moment
Sa pagkakaron – at this point in time
Karon – now
Niining orasa – at this time
Niining bahina – at this point

Let's take an illustration.

    Bakak – a lie (noun)
    Bakak – to lie (verb)

What forms can we get from this?
    Nibakak – has lied
    Namakak – lied
    Nagbakak – was lying
    Nagabakak – is lying
    Magbakak – will be lying
    Mamakak – will tell a lie
    Mobakak – will be telling a lie
    Nanghimakak – was dismissing as a lie
    Mihimakak – has dismissed as a lie
    Mohimakak – will dismiss as a lie
    Manghimakak – will be dismissing as a lie

Familiarize Yourself With These Common Prefixes

Gi

    Gi-among-amongan (was raped, root word: among-among/to violate)
    *Gi*buhat (was made or done, root word: buhat/deed)
    *Gi*dala (was brought, root word: dala/to bring)
    *Gi*dapit (was invited, root word: dapit/invite)
    Gi-ingon nga (was said to be, root word: ingon/to say as such)
    Gi-inom (was drank, root word: inom/to drink)
    *Gi*kuyogan (was accompanied, root word: kuyog/to accompany)
    *Gi*pangulo-han (was headed by, root word: ulo/head)
    *Gi*pasanginlan (was accused, root word: pasangil/accusation)
    *Gi*pusil (was shot, root word: pusil/to shoot)
    *Gi*sagol (was mixed, root word: sagol/to mix)
    *Gi*saway (was criticized, root word: sayaw/to critic)
    *Gi*subay (was checked, root word: subay/to trace)
    *Gi*tagsa-tagsa (was itemized, root word: taga usa/by one)
    *Gi*tanggong (was held captive, imprisoned)

*Gi*tinguha (was aspired, root word: kuha/to get)
*Gi*tubag (was answered, root word: tubag/answer)
*Gi*tuho-an (was believed, root word: tu-o/to heed)

Gika

*Gika*guol (has caused sorrow)
*Gika*subo (has been the cause of sorrow)
*Gika*takda (has been scheduled)

Gipa

*Gipa*higayon (was held)
*Gipa*hugtan (was tightened through)
*Gipa*mugos (was forced on)
Gipa-ubos (was ordered, was lowered)
Gipa-undang (was stopped)

Ipa

*Ipa*hibawo (to let everyone know)
*Ipa*mugos (to insist; to force on)
Ipasulod (to put inside)

Ma

Ma-ila (to identiffy)
*Ma*kita (to see)
*Ma*kuha (to achieve)
*Ma*tago (to hide)
*Ma*tandog (to be emotionally touched, to be in an altered state)
*Ma*tang-tang (to get fired, to be let go)
*Ma*tino (to find out)

Mag

*Mag*dagan (to run)
*Mag*sayaw (to dance)
*Mag*suka (to throw up)
*Mag*suot (to wear)

Maka

Makahipos (to be able to save)
Maka-inom (to be able to drink)
Maka-uli (to be able to go home)

Makdungog (to be able to hear)

Mi
- *Mi-a*gi (passed)
- *Mi*babag (stopped)
- *Mi*butyag (revealed)
- *Mi-*ingon (said)
- *Mi*sumbong (reported)
- *Mi*suway (tried)

Na
- *Na*himo (became)
- *Na*hitabo (happened)
- *Na*kuha (got)
- *Na*priso (jailed)
- *Na*sayud (knew)
- *Na*tubag (answered)
- *Na*tumba (fell)

Nag
- *Nag*duda (was suspicious)
- *Nag-e*dad (Aged at)
- *Nag*kinahanglan (needed)
- *Nag*lakaw (was walking)
- *Nag*puyo (lived)
- *Nag*silbi (served)
- *Nag*suporta (supported)
- *Nag*trabaho (worked)

Nagpa
- *Nagpa-*abang (has rented)
- *Nagpa*guyod (has allowed to be dragged)
- *Nagpa-*ila (has introduced)
- *Nagpa*salamat (has thanked)
- *Nagpa*tawag (has called up on)

Nagpaka
- *Nagpaka-*aron-ingnon (pretend, 'so someone will say' literal)
- *Nagpaka*buang (was into, engaged in)

*Nagpaka*buta-bungol (acted blind and deaf, in a state of being mindless, not concerned, turning a deaf ear)

Naka
    Naka-angkon (achieved, root word: angkon/to own)
    *Naka*bantay (noticed, root word: bantay/to guard)
    *Naka*gawas (freed, root word: gawas/outside)
    *Naka*hukom (has decided)
    *Naka*lingkod (has taken post)
    *Naka*mata (was awakened)
    *Naka*suway (has tried)

Nang
    *Nang*hilabot (gossiped)
    *Nang*hipos (cleaned up)
    *Nang*huwam (borrowed)
    Na-ngita (looked for)
    Na-ngutana (asked)

Nanga
    *Nanga*bu-ang (simultaneously gone crazy)
    Nangapukan (collectively taken)
    *Nanga*taktak (collectively dropped or fired)

Ni
    *Ni*bati (felt)
    *Ni*himo (did)

Nipa
    *Nipa*mando (has given order)
    *Nipa*saka (has raised)
    *Nipa*salig (has promised)
    *Nipa*silong (has taken shelter)
    *Nipa*tubag (has demanded an answer)

Pa
    *Pa*dagkutan (to have lighted)
    *Pa*pintalan (to have painted)
    *Pa*puli-han (to have replaced)
    *Pa*sudlan (to have filled)

Pag
    *Pag*lingkod (the taking of oath of office)
    *Pag*pamusil (the shooting)
        *Pag*paningkamot (the act of exerting effort)
        *Pag*pasar (the act of passing)

Did You Know This?

1. *Gayud, gyud, jud* mean the same thing.

2. Altered order and the forms pronouns take

   Dili *ko* na (I can't any longer)
   Dili na *nako (I no longer can)*

   Ang atong mga anak (our children)
   Ang mga anak nato (the children of ours)

   Sa atong nasud (of our nation)
   Sa nasud nato (of the nation that's ours)

   Usa ka enhinyero ako (An engineer, I am)
   Ako usa ka enhinyero (I am an engineer)

3. Suffixes 'hon' or 'on' *versus* prefix 'i' in verbs
   Eduka-hon – will educate
   i-edukar – going to educate

   Ato nga eduka-hon ang atong mga anak.
   We will educate our children.

   Atong i-edukar ang atong mga anak.
   We are going to educate our children.

   Iyang saulog-on ang iyang adlaw'ng natawhan.
   She will celebrate her natal day.

Iyang i-saulog ang iyang adlaw'ng natawhan.
She is going to celebrate her natal day.

4. 'Pinaka' used as a shortened form for 'pinaka katapusan' (the last)
   Pinaka sinsilyo – pinaka katapusan nga sinsilyo
   (the last penny)

   Pinaka hangyo – pinaka katapusan nga hangyo
   (the last request)

   Pinaka tulo – pinaka katapusang tulo
       (the last drop)

   Iya'ng pinakapangandoy – iyang pinaka katapusang pangandoy
       (his last wish)

The use of 'pinaka' in the context of most, best, worst and the superlative will be tackled in a later lesson.

5. 'Mas' can be used to mean better or more in a comparison.
   Mas mahal – more expensive
   Mas maayo – better
   Mas lagum – darker
   Mas malampuson – more successful

   Also, remember the use of the word 'kay sa' to mean 'compared to' or 'than'

   Mas barato kay sa – cheaper than
   Mas praktikal kay sa – more practical compared to
   Mas delikado kay sa – more dangerous than

6. Use of the concatenated 'ay' as a word helper.
   Ikaw mao ang tigdumala
   Ikaw mao'y tigdumala (you are the facilitator)
   Ika'y tigdumala (you are the facilitator)

   Ako aduna ay kwarta
   Ako aduna'y kwarta (I have money)

Wala ko ay kasayuran
Wala ko'y kasayuran (I have no knowledge)

Wala ay sapatos
Way sapatos (no shoes)

Naa ako ay paniudto
Naa ko'y paniudto (I have lunch)
Naa'y paniudto (there is lunch)

Chapter 7

Immersion Into the Cebuano (Visayan) Language

Challenge Your Comprehension

hat do these phrases mean? Come on, you got this!

Dili katuho-an nga mga panghitabo sa kalibutan.

Inig ka puti sa uwak.

Kapoy ba nimo oy.

Kuwang ang plete.

Langas kaayo ka.

Nganong magsige man jud ka ug samok nako?

Masakiton ka ba?

Matagamtaman nimo ang pinaka-anindot nga talan-awon.

Mona-ug ko sa eskina.

Nag madaugon siya.

Ngano ka?

Nganong dili ka magpadoktor?

Palayo, paduol!

Sayo sa buntag.

Sige ra ka nga wala diri.

Sige ra ka ug ka-uwahi.

Unsa na gud ni?

Be Curious

Can you answer the following questions?

1. What is the shortest word that you know in Cebuano?
2. What's the longest word that you know?
3. What is your favorite phrase?
4. What is your least favorite one?
5. What is the most confusing word that you have encountered in Cebuano?
6. What phrase do you know in Visayan that doesn't make sense?

Where do you hear these phrases?

Can you make sense of the following Cebuano (Visayan) phrases? Where are you most likely to encounter these? Hospital? Church? Street Corner? Market? School? Church? Or when in trouble with the law? Test your inner linguist.

1. Adto didto ang nauganan.
2. Ayaw pangopya sa imong silingan.
3. Ang Ginoo maga-uban kaninyo.
4. Ang pagkunhod sa panginahanglan sa trabahador.
5. Atong obserbahan ang kahilom sa panahon sa eksaminasyon.
6. Nisaka ang presyo sa bugas.

7. Sabta ang inyong leksyon.
8. Tikasan ang timbangan sa mga palitonon.
9. Ania ang mga biktima nga imong gikawatan.
10. Atimanon ka sa pinakamaayo nga doktor.
11. Atong lig-onon ang atong pagsalig sa Ginoo kay siya lang ang nasayud.
12. Atong sibugan bi, kay walo-walo ni.
13. Dali na!
14. Di na nako maantus ang ka-sakit.
15. Dili sayon ang akong kurso.
16. Dili masiguro ang kinabuhi apan ayaw pagpakawala sa pagla-um.
17. Dili kini moagi didto sa plaza.
18. Hinlo ba ang imong konsensya?
19. Huwat sa gud.
20. Ikaduhang eskina lang Manoy.
21. Nagkinahanglan siya ug dugo nga i-abuno alang sa operasyon.
22. Palit na kamo! Lab-as nga isda ug utanon.
23. Magbayad ka sa imong mga kasal-anan nga nabuhat.
24. Magtingkagol ka sa bilanggo-an.
25. Walay hangyo Manang?
26. Paningkamot nga mobalik ang kahimsog sa imong panglawas.
27. Nag kalapok nga kadalanan ang imong agi-an.
28. Siya napamatud-an nga nagagunit ug ginadili nga droga.
29. Kinahanglan ang pag-angkon ug lantip nga kaisipan.
30. Pasaylo-a ang imong mga kaaway.
31. Atong tumanon ang kasugu-an sa Diyos.
32. Palihug ug tunol ini dong.
33. Panglakaw kamo ug dad-a ang kalinaw sa Ginoo.
34. Sikitan nato gamay bi.
35. Sukli unya palihug.

Chapter 8

Functionality in Translation

n a culture, the language is build up by influences from visitors and from global media sources. Advances in business and technology also greatly affect the evolution of a language.

With this knowledge, the language of a nation or group of islands or tribe and its existence will withstand the changes for as long as it is able to preserve the indigenous treasure of the language origin and be able to adapt as well to new words.

I cannot say for sure that in the Cebuano (Visayan) culture, much has changed since then. The locale still chose to speak in the dialect, and on occasion will probably borrow some foreign words here and there.

But how do you form words for modern terminologies?

How do you break down an English word for example, so you can express it in the dialect?

I thought hard on this and the only way I could teach you to do it is based on what I have learned growing up in the Philippines.

During my early childhood days, electricity was just introduced. We were basically burning gas lamps fueled by kerosene which we all refer to as 'gas' in our dialect. When electricity was introduced we learn new words like 'wire', 'transformer', 'fluorescent lamp', 'electric bulb', 'electrical outlet', 'stereo speakers', 'electrical cord', 'radio', etc.

So, do you express these new words in dialect?

Is it even necessary to convert these words into its Visayan counterpart?

The answer is Yes and No.

Yes, you do have the option to express these words in dialect.

No. It is not necessary to translate them.

You can however express them in dialect to maintain the organic potential of the words.

But just a word of caution. Be reasonable about when you really need to translate them, and ask yourself, "Will the translation make better sense?"

In all its essence, language in any form is a tool – a tool of expression to communicate to understand and be understood.

And perhaps that is the basic concept of why and when we need to translate words.

We as a group of speaking mammals want to have a collective understanding of the language that we use to communicate with each other.

'Wire' for example if understood can be said as is, just the foreign word 'wire', and I am referring to the electrical wire.

Else, a description of what a wire looks or does is needed.

What is a wire? Typically, it is a piece of copper wrapped in an insulated material.

I can say 'usa ka'(a piece of) 'bronse'(bronze or copper) 'nga giputos' (that is wrapped) 'sa usa ka'(in an) 'di maka-kuryente' (something that will not electrify, in other words insulated) 'nga materyal' (material)

Thus,

'usa ka bronse nga giputos ug di maka-kuryente nga materyal'

Means I am referring to a wire.

In this case we learn to just say, wire. Why? It is the most functional approach.

I don't think we have a word for 'transformer' either. We used to get power outage from overloaded transformers in the main electrical lines powering the many houses.

We simply say,
    Nibuto ang transformer. (The transformer exploded.)

Ang transformer ni-buto. (The transformer exploded.)

We call the fluorescent lamp or bulb simply as,
> Flo-re-sent (fluorescent) (and enunciating the sound is more important than the spelling sometimes)

Electric bulb is,
> Bombilya sa suga (bulb is 'bombilya')

Electrical outlet or electrical socket is,
> Pansakanan sa kuryente
> Pansakanan (an object where you can 'pansak' or insert something)
> Kuryente (general term for current or electricity)

Electrical line is,
> Linya sa kuryente

Electrical post is,
> Poste sa suga ('Suga' is general term for lamp)

Stereo speaker has no equivalent but the closest I could think of is
> Panghaw nga steryo ('panghaw' is the speaker system)

Electrical cord is simply,
> Kord sa kuryente

Cassette tape,
> Ka-set teyp (We borrow the pronunciation without translating)

Radio is,
> Radyo

Radio station,
> Estasyon sa radio

AM or FM radio stations,
> Maminaw ug drama ug balita sa AM (To listen to drama programs and news at the AM station)
> Maminaw ug musika sa FM (To listen to music at the FM station)

Battery is,
> Baterya sa radyo (the small batteries)
> Baterya sa sakyanan (the humungous battery used in vehicles)

What I am trying to impart here is that the way we translate is highly dependent on our need to convey or express an idea, and sometimes when we can't find a more precise description of that idea we simply borrow the foreign word as is, for functionality.

Just try to imagine me warning somebody for safety and I must express the word 'wire' in the most indigenous way.

That would be tantamount to saying,

Palayo diha sa 'usa ka bronse nga giputos ug di maka-kuryente nga materyal' kay basin makuryente ka!

It is not as practical as,
Palayo diha sa 'wire' kay basin makuryente ka!

Which basically means,
Stay away from the 'wire' because you might get electrocuted!
(unless of course the person I'm talking to does not understand wire.)

Later on, we learned to use 'alambre' for wire but the kind that is not insulated or just the copper wire underneath a typical wire.

In closing, let me give you a very common approach of translating words based on functions:

Kalibangan (bathroom, comfort room or CR)
Root word: libang/to move bowel

Tugpahanan sa eroplano (airport)
Root word: tugpa/to land
Root word: eroplano/airplane

Sakyanang pangkawanangan (airplane, vehicle on air)
Root word: sakyanan (vehicle)
Root word: wanang (expanse or air space)
Thus,
Airport – tugpahanan sa sakyanang pangkawanangan

Other examples:
Tindahan (store)
Root word: tinda/sell

Baligya-anan (market)
Root word: baligya/trade or sell

Kan-anan (a table or a restaurant or a place to eat)
Root word: kaon/eat

Abtanan (a meeting place)
Root word: mag-abot/to meet

Hunonganan sa mga sakyanan (Stopping area for vehicles)
Root word: Hunong/stop

Nauganan sa mga pasahero (Disembarking area for passengers)
Root word: Naug/to go down or alight from a vehicle

Katulganan (a place or spot to sleep on)
Root word: tulog/sleep

Pamantalaan (newspaper)
Root word: mantala (to publish or to disseminate information)

Pasilonganan (a place to seek shelter or seek help)
Root word: Pasilong/take shelter

Hulganan (a spot to drop things into; drop box)
Root word: hulog/to drop
Hulganan sa suwat (mailbox)
Hulganan sa tabang (donation box)
Hulganan sa mga reklamo (complaints box)
Hulganan sa suhestiyon (suggestion box)

Another word for box is 'kahon'.

Sapatosan (shoes section)
Root word: sapatos/shoes

Sinina-an (dress area)
Root word: sinina /dress

Ilisanan (changing area)
Root word: ilis/to change

Ilisanan sa kwarta (money exchange place)
Ilisanan sa dolyar (dollar exchange place)

Sinehan (movie house)
Root word: Sine/movie

Prisohan (jail)
Root word: priso/to hold captive

Tadtaran (chopping block)
Root word: tadtad/to chop

Sayawanan (dance floor)
Root word: sayaw/to dance

Basurahan (Garbage bin)
Root word: basura/trash

Bulangan (a place where derby is held)
Root word: bulang/to hold a match or competition

Sugalan (casino or a place of gamble)
Root word: sugal/place a bet or gamble

Tambalanan (hospital)
Root word: tambal/medicine

Alampo-anan (a place of worship)
Root word: ampo/to pray

I hope you get the idea here. If you hear any word that has the 'anan' or 'an' suffix it is probably a derivative noun created by transforming the root word.

In the same manner you can play with the English words you know and learn to convert them to the Cebuano (Visayan) language.

Say,
    A place to hide (hide in Cebuano is 'tago')
Thus,
    Tago-anan (is a spot where you can hide)
Or,
    A vacation spot (vacation is 'bakasyon' in Cebuano)
So,

Bakasyonan (is a vacation destination)

What about a person or something that you can use to vent sadness or pent up emotions with?

The root word in Visayan is 'pahungaw' which means to air out or let steam out or to vent.

So, you can say,

Pahungawanan – is the person or the getaway or the escape

Ikaw maoy akong pahungawanan. (You are my confidante.)

Ikaw maoy akong pahungawanan sa akong mga kaguol. (You are the person whom I can share my sadness with.)

Let's Translate:

Sports is my escape to vent out all my frustrations.

Sports – pa-ugnat sa kusog
My escape to vent out – pahungawanan
All – tanan
My (possessive) – nako nga - nakong
Frustrations – kapungot (root word: pungot/angry)

Thus, in Cebuano (Visayan)

Ang pa-ugnat sa kusog may akong pahungawanan sa tanan nakong kapungot.

I hope that as you go along on learning the language, you can become a master of deducing the root words and prefixing and suffixing them to come up with another word that still carries the core meaning of the word.

Chapter 9

Aspire to Translate to Inspire

Say It Differently, But Say It Right

id you sometimes wish that you know every synonym or antonym of every word, so you can convey every thought with eloquence?

This section covers translation of phrases. Take note of the underlined words of the translated phrases in Cebuano. Those words are the alternative way of stating the word or words, while keeping the same or similar context.

1. A good heart deserves a good home.
    Ang maayo nga kasing-kasing – a good heart
    Angayan sa - deserves
    Maayo nga puloy-anan – a good home

   Ang ma-ayo nga kasing-kasing <u>angayan sa</u> ma-ayo nga puloy-anan.
   Ang ma-ayo nga kasing-kasing <u>takos sa</u> ma-ayo nga puloy-anan.

2. When you are happy with who you are, it doesn't matter who isn't.
    Kung malipayon ka – when you are happy
    Sa imong pagkatawo – with who you are
    Dili na importante – it doesn't matter
    Kung kinsa ang wala (nalipay.) – who isn't (happy)

   Kung <u>malipayon</u> ka sa imong pagkatawo <u>dili na importante</u> kung <u>kinsa ang wala</u>.
   Kung <u>nalipay</u> ka sa imong pagkatawo <u>dili importante</u> kung <u>kinsa ang wala nalipay</u>.

3. When the right door opens, you can walk through it with ease.

Kung moabri ang tukma nga pwertahan – when the right door opens
Makasulod ka niini – you can walk through it
With ease – sa tumang kasayon.

Kung <u>mo-abri</u> ang <u>tukma</u> nga <u>pwertahan</u> <u>makasulod</u> ka niini sa <u>tumang</u> kasayon.
Kung <u>mo-abli</u> ang <u>sakto</u> nga <u>pultahan</u> <u>makasud</u> ka niini sa <u>labing</u> kasayon.

4. Treat each day like the gift that it is, with love, compassion, optimism.
   Amumaha – Treat
   Ang matag adlaw – each day

   Susama sa usa ka regalo – like a gift
   Nga mao kini – that it is
   Uban sa gugma – with love
   Pagkamapuanguron - compassion
   Masaligon nga pagtuo – faith (optimism)

   <u>Amumaha</u> *ang <u>matag</u> adlaw <u>susama</u> sa usa ka <u>regalo</u> nga mao kini,*
   <u>Alimahi</u> *ang <u>kada</u> adlaw <u>pareha</u> sa usa ka <u>gasa</u> nga mao kini,*

   Uban sa gugma, <u>pagkamapuanguron</u>, <u>masaligon nga pagtuo</u>.
   Uban sa gugma, <u>pakigdait</u>, <u>pagsalig</u>.

5. Live a meaningful life.
   Puy-i – Live
   Ang mapahimuslanon nga kinabuhi – meaningful life

   Puy-i ang <u>mapahimuslanon</u> nga kinabuhi.
   Puy-i ang <u>makahuloganon</u> nga kinabuhi.

6. Don't judge what people do until you know what they've been through.
   Ayaw hukmi – don't judge
   Ang binuhatan sa usa ka tawo – what people do
   Hangtud nga imong masayran – until you know
   Kung unsa ang ilang na-agi-an (sa kinabuhi) – what they've been through (in life)

   Ayaw hukmi ang <u>binuhatan sa usa ka tawo</u>,

Ayaw hukmi ang <u>kinabuhi sa uban</u>,

Hangtud nga imong <u>masayran</u> kung unsa ang ilang <u>na-agi-an</u> (sa kinabuhi.)
Hangtud nga imong <u>masabtan</u> kung unsa ang ilang <u>nasinati</u> (sa kinabuhi.)

7. There's a price for everything. To create you must destroy.
    Adunay tugbang – there's a price
    Alang sa matag butang – for everything
    Kung maghimo ka ug bag-o – to create
    Kinahanglan ka nga moguba – to destroy

    Adunay <u>tugbang</u> alang sa <u>matag</u> butang.
    Adunay <u>balor</u> alang sa <u>kada</u> butang.

    Kon <u>magmugna</u> ka (ug bag-o), kinahanglan <u>nimo nga gub-on</u> (ang daan.)
    Kon <u>maghimo</u> ka (ug bag-o), kinahanglan <u>ka nga muguba</u> (sa daan.)

8. What we achieve inwardly will change outer reality.
    Unsa ang atong ma-angkon – what we achieve
    Sa ilawom – inwardly
    Mo-usab – will change
    Sa panggawas nga reyalidad – outer reality

    Unsa ang atong <u>ma-angkon</u> sa <u>ilawom</u>
    Unsa ang atong <u>makab-ot</u> sa <u>kina-iladman</u>

    <u>*Mo-usab*</u> *sa <u>panggawas nga reyalidad</u>.*
    <u>*Mo-bag-o*</u> *sa <u>reyalidad nga atong matagamtaman</u>.*

9. You are magic. Know that you are magic, and no one can stop you.
    Usa ikaw ka mahika – You are magic
    Hibaw-i kana – Know that
    Ug wala'y makapugong kanimo – and no one can stop you

    <u>*Usa ikaw ka mahika*</u>*.*
    <u>*Makagagahum ka*</u>*.*

    <u>*Hibaw-i*</u> *kana.*
    <u>*Hinumdomi*</u> *kana.*

Ug wala'y makapugong kanimo.
Ug wala'y makapahunong kanimo.

10. The moment you get comfortable, you are doomed.
    Sa higayon – the moment
    (nga) mahimo kang komportable (sa imong kahimtang) – when you get comfortable
    Ikaw ala-ut. – you are doomed

    Sa higayon nga mahimo kang komportable (sa imong kahimtang), ikaw ala-ut.
    Sa pag-abot sa panahon nga makontento ka, demalas ka.

More Practice Translations

Let's play around with the following phrases.

1. <u>To err</u> is human, <u>to forgive</u> is divine.
   Ang pagpakasala tawhanon, ang pagpasaylo bala-anon.

   How did we arrive at this translation?
   Sala – sin (Cebuano)
   Pagpakasala – act of sinning (root word: sala/sin)
   Tawhanon – of human nature (root word: tawo/human being)
   Pasaylo – forgive (Cebuano)
   Pagpasaylo – act of forgiving (root word: pasaylo/forgiveness)
   Bala-anon – holy (root word: Bala-an/holy)

2. Learn to turn the <u>other cheek</u>.
   Makat-on nga mo-tunol sa pikas nga aping.

Translation Guide:
   Makat-on – to learn (root word: kat-on/learn)
   Molihay – to move from one side to the other (root word: tunol/to hand)

Sa pikas – the other side
Aping – Cheek

Now it's your turn. Identify the translation for the underlined English word(s).

1. It is <u>better</u> to light a candle than to <u>curse</u> the darkness.
    Mas maayo nga magdagkot ug kandila kaysa imong panghimara-uton ang kangitngit.

2. Peace <u>comes</u> from loving every part of <u>your journey</u>, even the <u>dark places</u>.
    Ang kalinaw nagagikan sa paghigugma sa matag parte sa imong paglawig, bisan sa mga ngitngit nga lugar.

3. We <u>fall in love</u> with <u>the struggle</u> and the pains that <u>force us</u> to learn and <u>evolve</u>. In the end it is the process that we <u>truly</u> love.
    Mahigugma ta sa pag-antus ug sa sakit nga maoy motukmod kanato aron makat-on ug motubo. Sa kataposan, ang proseso mao gyud ang tinuod nato nga gihigugma.

4. <u>Let</u> it <u>go</u>. Turn <u>it</u> off. Walk away. Breathe.
    Buhi-i kini. Pawunga kini. Palayo niini. Ginhawa.

5. Love <u>yourself</u> like it is your <u>job</u>.
    Higugma-a ang imong kaugalingon nga mora ug imo kining trabaho.

6. The journey of <u>a thousand</u> miles <u>begin</u> with the <u>first step</u>.
    Ang biyahe sa usa ka libo nga milya nagasukad sa una nga lakang.

7. <u>Through</u> <u>inquiring</u> of the old <u>we learn</u> of the new.
    Pinaagi sa pagtugkad sa daan makat-onan nato ang bag-o.

8. If you <u>could be anybody</u> who would you be?
    Kung mahimo ikaw nga si bisan kinsa, kinsa ka?

9. Que sera, sera.
    Kung unsa man gani ang mahitabo, mahitabo.
    Bahala na.

Mastery Thru Practice

1. Mastering your awareness.
    Master – bansay
    Mastering – ang pagbansay
    Aware – sayud/kahibalo
    Awareness – kasayuran
    Ang pagbansay sa imong kasayuran.

2. Mastering your needs.
    Ang pagbansay sa imong panginahanglan.

3. Mastering your emotions.
    Ang pagbansay sa imong mga pagbati.

4. Mastering your communication.
    Ang pagbansay sa imong pakighinabi.
    Root word: tabi/chat; converse
    Alternate:
    Ang pagbansay sa imong pakig-istorya.
    Root word: istorya/talk

    Alternate 2:
    Ang pagbansay sa imong pakig-himamat.
    Root word: himamat/mingle; meet people

5. Mastering your purpose in life.
    Ang pagbansay sa imong katuyo-an sa kinabuhi.
    Root word: tuyo/aim

    Ang pagbansay – the act of mastering something
    Can be replaced with: Ang pagkahanas
    (Root word: hanas/expert)
    Pagkahanas: being an expert

6. Empowered state of consciousness
    Magamhanon – Empowered
    Root word: Gahum/power

Kahimtang – state
Kahibalo-an – Consciousness/Knowledge
Root word: hibalo; know
Kalamdagan – Enlightenment
Root word: light/lamdag
Magamhanong kahimtang sa kahibalo-an.
Magamhanong kahimtang sa kalamdagan.

7. Lay the foundation to a life that transcends tribulations.
Ang paghan-ay ug pundasyon alang sa usa ka kinabuhi nga maka buntog sa mga pagsuway.

    Root words:
    Han-ay – Lay
    Pundasyon – Foundation
    Alang – for
    Buntog – To overcome
    Pagsuway – Trials

Alternate:
Ang paghan-ay ug pundasyon alang sa usa ka kinabuhi nga makasagubang sa mga unos sa kinabuhi.

    Root words:
    Sagubang – Withstand
    Unos – storm
    Mga unos sa kinabuhi – life's storms (alternate for tribulations)

Chapter 10

When All Else Fails, Translate!

Have you seen the movie, "The God's Must Be Crazy!"

Well if you didn't, that funny movie featured an empty soda bottle that fell from the sky and the locals in that place thought it was some God that fell from heaven.

Assume for a second, that a similar scenario happened somewhere in a very remote island in one of the deepest unventured nooks in the Visayas region where no one speaks English. You were there, and though you speak English those natives don't.

An iPhone fell from the sky and the whole island panicked at the sight of this glowing magical piece of miracle or curse that fell from the sky. Chaos is about to ensue as fear gripped the whole tribe. The whole island will burn anything and anyone who touched that device.

Now your survival depends on how well you can translate and explain what the device does and the best way to do it is to give the chief of the tribe a walkthrough of the prompts on the screen.

And you can't fail. Your life depends on it.

Will you pass the challenge?

1. Categories - Mga Kategorya
2. Education - Edukasyon
3. Entertainment - Kalingawan
4. Finance – Pinansyal, Mahitungod sa Kwarta

5. Food and Drink – Pagkaon ug Ilim-non
6. Health and Fitness – Maayong Panglawas ug Kahimsug
7. Home and Auto – Balay ug Sakyanan
8. Lifestyle – Pagpuyo sa Kinabuhi
9. News - Balita
10. Productivity – Mapahimuslanong Pag-ugmad
11. Religion and Spirituality – Relihiyon ug Pagtuo (Spirtualidad)
12. Shopping - Pagkumpra
13. Sports – Paugnat sa Kusog
14. Travel - Pagsuroy
15. Suggested For You – Gisugyot Alang Kanimo
16. Recently Used – Pinaka-ulahi nga Nagamit
17. Featured – Mga Gipasi-ugdahan
18. Home – Nabigar Ngadto sa Pinakasinugdanan
19. People – Mga Tawo
20. Games – Mga Duwa
21. Discover – Diskobre-a
22. Sync Contacts – I-tukma ang Listahan sa Mga Kaila
23. Connect Instagram – I-dugtong ang Instagram
24. All Contacts – Tanan Nga Mga Kaila
25. Suggested People – Gisugyot nga Mga Tawo
26. Scan Code – Kuha-a ug Basaha ang Kodigo
27. Invite - Imbitaha
28. Requests – Mga Hangyo
29. Add - Idugang
30. Settings – Mga Aspeto ug Mga Lagda
31. Finish Setting Up Your Phone – Tapuson ug Han-ay ang mga Lagda sa Imong Telepono
32. Airplane Mode – Modo nga Pang-eroplano
33. Wi-Fi – Sinyas Nga Pinaagi sa Kahanginan
34. Bluetooth – Pagkutas sa Tingog Pina-agi sa Kahanginan
35. Cellular – Klase sa Sinyas sa Kahanginan nga Mapunit sa Mobilo o Mabitbit nga Telepono
36. Personal Hotspot – Kaugalingon nga Pagpakatap sa Mobilo nga Sinyas sa Kahanginan
37. Carrier – Ngalan sa Tigpasiugda sa Sinyas sa Kahanginan sa Imong Mabitbit nga Telepono
38. Notifications – Mga Pahibalo
39. Control Center – Sentro sa Pag-usab sa Lagda sa mga Aspeto sa Imong Pang-elektroniko nga Himan

40. Do not disturb – Ayaw ug Samoka
41. General – Tinanan nga Lagda
42. Display & Brightness – Hitsura ug ang Kahayagon
43. Wallpaper – Ang Pinakatabon
44. Sounds & Haptics – Lagda sa Mga Tingog ug Paghikam sa Mobilo nga Himan
45. Vibrate on Ring – Mokurog Inig Bagting
46. Vibrate on Silent – Mokurog Bisan Kung Gibutang sa Lagda nga Hilom
47. Change With Buttons – Bag-ohon Pinaagi sa mga Butones
48. Ringtone – Tingog Ini'g Bagting
49. Text Tone – Tingog Kon Adunay Bag-ong Teksto
50. New Voicemail – Bag-o nga Message Pina-agi sa Tingog
51. New Mail – Bag o nga Suwat
52. Sent Mail – Napadala nga Suwat
53. Calendar Alerts – Mga Pahimangno Nga Gi-base sa Kalendaryo
54. Reminder Alerts – Mga Pahimangno Ubay sa mga Pahinumdom
55. AirDrop – Pagbalhin sa mga Larawan ug Salida Pinaagi sa Kahanginan Gikan sa Usa Ka-himan Ngadto sa Lain
56. Keyboard Clicks – Kasikas sa Mapislit nga mga Butones Sa Kompyuter
57. Lock Sound – I-kandado ang Napili-an nga Tingog
58. System Haptics – Mga Lagda sa Sistema sa Paghikam sa Imong Elektroniko nga Himan

Ka-ubo!

The root word is 'ubo' which means cough. Ka-ubo means you coughed. But in this case, the word is used to denote the idea that someone choked hard while performing a difficult undertaking. You can pretty much say this word to tell someone how they got a taste of what they wished for.

The first time when I was doing the translation of the phrases above, I realized how hard it is to find the right word sometimes. Despite my wildly and widely equipped weaponry of words, every now and then I say to myself, 'Ka-ubo!' recognizing the level of difficulty when it comes to translating newly accepted English terms into the Cebuano (Visayan) lingo.

Gi-sunggo!

The root word is 'sunggo'. Sunggo is nosebleed. Thus, gi-sunggo is someone who had a nosebleed. In this case though, the expression is a hypothetical description of someone getting it from undergoing something so difficult. This is also a very common Cebuano expression.

It is used interchangeably with the former, 'Ka-ubo.'

Now if you want to really dig deeper into translation and see how many words can't be fully expressed in Cebuano, check social media and dig into the settings.

It is amazing to realize that, if there is no attempt to even document these things, any translation will probably do. The challenge of the translation is keeping it terse and accurate without being too literal. Armed with just a dictionary, it is fairly impossible to do the full translation at times. You have to understand the core word origin.

For example:
Bluetooth
    Blue – Asul
    Tooth – Ngipon

If you take this translation, asul nga ngipon, it doesn't mean anything at all. Thus, the more lengthy translation of what a Bluetooth does is more appropriate in this case.

Balik-Lantaw (A Look Back)

If you got a hold of the introductory book on Cebuano or Visayan that I authored earlier, you must have noticed that I keenly suggested to every reader about enriching himself with the Visayan literary treasure through some of the more popular Cebuano music. It was my conviction, that such works have innate beauty in their art that will help frame the preservation of the language over time.

Examine the following translations.

Usahay magadamgo ako
At times I dream

Nga ikaw ug ako *nagkahigugma-ay*
That you and I *fell in love with each other*

Matud nila
According to them

Ako *dili angay*
I am *not worthy*

Gugmang *putli*
Pure love

Mao ray bahandi
Is my *only* treasure

Maoy *bahandi* labaw sa *bulawan*
The only *treasure* more than *gold*

Matud mo ako imong *unungan*
According to you, you *will stay* with me

Mahalon, hangtud sa *lubnganan*
Be loved, until I'm in my *graveyard*

Pahaloka ko day
Let me kiss you girl

Asa man?
Where?

Sa imong *aping*
On your *cheek*

Aw diay!
Oh really!

I-hilak ko lang *sa tago*
I am going to cry *in silence*

Ang kasakit sa *kamingaw*
The pain of *loneliness*

If you were curious about learning and understanding Cebuano (Visayan) dialect, as I have suggested in my previous book, immersing yourself in the culture of the language is probably one of the easiest and most enjoyable ways to learn the dialect.

Let's tackle the verb use of the word 'damgo'
    Magadamgo – the act of dreaming (progressive)
    Nagdamgo (past tense) – Dreamed
    Modamgo (future tense) – To dream

Take the example:
    To dream the impossible dream.

Visayan translation:
    Ang pagdamgo sa imposible nga damgo.

Why not:
    Modamgo sa imposible nga damgo.
Explanation:

Most Visayan terms that are originally in verb format are easily converted to the noun equivalent by translating it as an act.

Pagdamgo – act of dreaming
Thus, to dream (or the act of dreaming) – Ang pagdamgo

The Use of the Prefix 'Pag' with a Verb

Check the following examples:

1. Ang pag*saka* sa presyo – the rise in prices (root word: saka/to go up)

2. Ang pag*kunhod* sa ani – the decrease in harvest (root word: kunhod/to decrease)

3. Ang pag*salig* sa isig ka tawo – the trust between fellowmen (root word: salig/to trust)

4. Ang wala'y pag*hunong* sa ulan – the continuous pouring of the rain (root word: hunong/to stop) (here: wala makes the verb, 'to not stop)

5. Ang *pag-amuma* sa imong hinigugma – your lover's nourishing (root word: amuma/to take care)

6. Ang *pagsaulog* sa adlaw'ng natawhan – the celebration of your day of birth (root word: saulog/to celebrate)

7. Ang *pagsud-ong* sa imong kalampusan – to witness your success (root word: sud-ong/to view)

8. Ang *pagpahimulos* sa akong kaayo – to abuse my goodness (root word: pahimulos/to take advantage)

9. Ang *pagbasul* sa imong sala – the repentance of your sins (root word: basul/to repent)

10. Ang pagtapos sa iyang kurso – the completion of his course (root word: tapos/to finish)

Observe carefully how the root 'verb' or root action word is transformed into a noun by using 'pag' to mean the act of 'doing something.'

Use of the Prefix 'Pagka' When a Verb is Used Indirectly

1. Ang *pagka*pawong sa sugang dagitabnon – the loss of electricity (root word: pawong/to shut off)

2. Ang *pagka*hugno sa tulay – the collapse of the bridge (root word: hugno/to fall)

Lesson:
The resulting word with the prefix is also a noun – loss, collapse

The difference is that, the root verbs were used in an indirect statement of an object.
That is, electricity was shut off. - *napawong*
(What was shut off? The electricity.)

The bridge has fallen. - *nahugno*
(What has fallen? The bridge.)

If that sounds confusing, this lesson is touching on English grammar for the reason of structure.
The one thing that you need to remember is that if you see a word starting with 'pag', 'pagka' it is most likely a derived noun from an action word especially if it is preceded by the word 'ang' (the) in a sentence or statement.

The Prefix 'Pagka' With an Adjective

An adjective is a word that describes something – jealous, rich, filthy

The examples given here uses 'pagka' with an adjective or descriptive word and the resulting context is that of a noun.

The use of 'pagka' is meant to describe 'a state of something'

1. Ang pagkaselosa sa imong asawa – the jealousy of your wife (root word: selosa/jealous)

2. Ang pagkahugawan sa imong anak – your child's filthy tendencies (root word: hugawan/filthy)

3. Ang pagka-adunahan sa ilang pamilya – their family's affluence (root word: adunahan/rich)

Cebuano Expressions: Eskina lang!

You will hear these words often. Some of them are considered vulgar slang. Know and understand them. Let's call them 'kanto words'. 'Kanto' means corner or in other words 'eskina'.

1. Atay ba nimo oy!
2. Lisura oy!
3. Paksit gyud!
4. Gago!
5. Iring!
6. Iring gibangas!

7. Gibangkong na!
8. Char!
9. Charot!
10. Angal ka?
11. Ahak gyud nimo!
12. Bungkag lapinig!
13. Sumpay-tina-e!
14. Nagmata ug buntag!
15. Way-si! (way siguro)
16. Usob pay layog!
17. Kakha-tuka!
18. Kaon-kalibang!
19. Buang!
20. Diretso lang!
21. Yabag!
22. Nawong ug sapi.
23. Pobre pa's manghihilot.
24. Ala-ut gyud.
25. Patis!
26. Yabo!
27. Tiwas!
28. Tomas! (Samot)
29. Eskina lang.
30. Lugar lang.
31. Sige.
32. Lagi ba.
33. Ha?
34. Unsa?
35. Samok!
36. Taym sa.
37. Ngari bi.
38. Huwat ba.
39. Sunggo!
40. Kaubo!

Words That Seem Hard to Translate

Words become challenging to translate when there is no one word that can be used in its stead. A good example is the word best.

If I say to you,

'You are the best.'

This phrase can arrive at several translations in Visayan because it can't be translated without the aid of another word. Informally, you can say,

'Ikaw na gyud.'

Or

'Ikaw na.'

But this translation does not embody the essence of saying 'you are the best' be it to your child, your mother, your husband, your friend, or your lover.

Best – Pinaka

She is the *best dancer* at the ball.
Siya ang *pinaka maayo mosayaw* didto sa pagsaulog.

Life is the *best teacher* that you can find.
Ang kinabuhi mao ang *pinaka maayo nga magtutudlo* nga imong makaplagan.

The *best prayer* is gratitude.
Ang *pinaka maayo nga pag-ampo* mao ang pagpasalamat.

You can find the *best and most beautiful beaches* in the Philippine islands.
Imong makaplagan *ang pinakamaayo ug pinakanindot nga mga baybayon* sa mga isla sa Pilipinas.

The *best* is yet to come.
Ang *pinakanindot* (nga butang), uma-abot pa lamang.

The *best years of my life* happened when I was with you.
Ang *pinakanindot nga mga katuigan sa akong kinabuhi* nahitabo sa panahon nga ako uban kanimo.

From what you can see, the word *best* needs another word to complete the thought when translated. The words that can be used to express the full essence is dependent on the whole context of the phrase or statement. The same holds true for the word *most*.

Most – *Pinaka*

You are the *most beautiful girl* in the world.
Ikaw ang *pinaka gwapa nga babaye* sa tibuok kalibutan.

Your sister is the *most cunning person* that I ever knew.
Ang imong igsoong babaye maoy *pinaka dautan nga tawo* nga akong nailhan.

This might be the *most thrilling* adventure of my life.
Mao na tingali kini ang *pinaka kulba hinam nga kaagi* nga akong natagamtaman sa akong kinabuhi.

LESSON:
Aside from 'most' and 'best' or 'worst', any superlative connotation in English uses the word 'pinaka' when translated.

the *happiest* people – ang *pinaka malipayon* nga mga tawo
the *richest* country – ang *pinaka datu* nga nasud
the *ugliest* trait – ang *pinaka bati* nga kinaiya
the *deepest* ocean – ang *pinaka lawom* nga dagat
the *silliest* comment – ang *pinaka wala'y hinungdan* nga komento
the *sweetest* smile – ang *pinaka tam-is* nga pahiyum
the *ugliest* creature – ang *pinaka ngil-ad* nga binuhat
the *hardest* words – ang *pinaka lisud* nga mga pulong

Say It in Cebuano

1. A teen girl - Dalagita
2. A young lady - Dalaga
3. About - Bahin
4. After - Human
5. Again - Gihapon
6. At the corner - Sa may eskina
7. Based on - Base sa
8. Because of - Tungod sa
9. Before - Una
10. Case of - Kaso nga
11. Dawn - Kaadlawon
12. From the - Gikan sa
13. From the other night – Sa miagi nga gabii
14. Go on - Padayon
15. In such case - Sa maong kaso
16. In the past - Kaniadto
17. It was not - Wala diay tuod
18. Just recently - Bag-ohay pa lang
19. Last month of April - Niadtong buwan sa Abril
20. More than a year ago - Kapin usa ka tuig na nga milabay
21. Not so long ago - Dili pa lang dugay
22. Now - Karon
23. Of this city - Ni-ining dakbayan or Ning dakbayan
24. Past eight in the morning – Pasado alas otso sa buntag
25. Shot dead - Gipusil patay
26. Since – Sanglit or Tungod kay
27. So - Aron
28. Thus – Mao nga or Maong
29. This year - Ning tuiga
30. Unidentified - Wala mailhi

31. Was at the place - Nga miadto sa lugar
32. Was - Maoy
33. When - Sa diha nga
34. While - Samtang
35. Yesterday - Kagahapon

Chapter 11

Bohol: The Land Without A Horse (Kabayo)

Speak Boholano

I don't expect you to know this, but there is a famous quip that says, there is no 'kabayo' (horse) in Bohol.

And it's very true.

Bohol is a neighboring island of Cebu. You can easily take a fast craft from Cebu to Bohol in roughly thirty minutes in a calm weather. That's how I used to remember it.

Bohol is famous for the Chocolate Hills, the floating Loboc River restaurant, and the Philippine tarsier, a small insect-feeding nocturnal primate with the cutest googly eyes.

Bohol is close to my heart. My grandparents are from Bohol. Most of my extended family also reside in Bohol.

My one absolute favorite is the 'calamay' (dialect for sugar). Calamay is not just sugar though. It is a delicacy made with coconut milk, ground sticky white rice, and red unrefined sugar cooked into a sticky consistency and packed in a skillfully polished pair of empty coconut shells and usually sealed using a red-colored paper tape. You get the picture, right? These are usually sold at the port area of Tagbilaran.

Red rice, anyone? Oh yes, I remember how good the red rice is. It is more like a variant of the typical brown rice, but only so much better.

Tagbilaran is the business hub of Bohol but in present-day settings, Panglao island has attracted so much of the business. You want to find an alternative of Boracay? Then go to Panglao island. There is an abundance of top-rated resorts that can cater to your traveling needs.

There is also a rise in the number of dining places to choose from, especially for expats and other foreign visitors to the island.

You can also easily catch a flight to Manila from Tagbilaran.

Farming and fishing as with the other neighboring Visayan islands is the primary source of income for most family units. A good number of Boholanos are also overseas workers.

The island has a nice little character on its own. People are friendly, and you can pretty much go around easily in a tricycle (a public transportation alternative) or you can also rent a car for ease of travel with air conditioning options during hot (which is normal weather) days.

Bohol is known for housing one of the oldest landmarks in Philippine history. The famous Loboc Church is one of them.

So, after all that lengthy introduction, let me get back to my original narrative.

No horses in Bohol, huh?

Yes. Absolutely. The kind of horse that Cebuanos and other Visayans know – kabayo.

This is a joke. But it's a good one.

This joke will help you remember that for so long as you can speak or understand Visayan, you pretty much can speak Boholano.

Boholano is just a slight variant of Cebuano or Visayan dialect.

What is the difference?

The 'y' (read as the word 'why') sound in Cebuano changes to a 'j' sound in Boholano. Similar to the end sound when you read the word 'edge' /edj/.

Thus,

> Kabayo (horse in Cebuano) – Kabajo (horse in Boholano)
> Kayo (fire in Cebuano) – kajo (fire in Boholano)

Other Examples:
> Ayaw baya hikalimti – Please do not forget
> Ajaw baja hikalimti – Please do not forget
> Nisayaw ang babaye – The girl danced
> Nisajaw ang baje – The girl danced
> Dili ko mokuyog – I am not coming
> Di ko mokujog – I am not coming

There are more words but this premise of the 'y' to 'j' sound is pretty much the very basic concept of adapting Cebuano dialect to Boholano. And like all rules, there are always exceptions. Not all words with 'y' sound in it will be converted to the 'j'-sounding Boholano equivalent.

Most words that end in 'y' remain the same, like balay (house), sudlay (comb), aguroy (an expression).

If you go to Bohol and you speak in Cebuano or Visayan, without the 'j' accent, you will still be understood.

A more famous Boholano phrase is the:

> Ija-ija, ahu-aho (/i-dya/ /i-dya/ /a-huh/ /a-hoh/)

Note: The 'j' soung is pronounced with a 'dya' as in the English word 'jar' and not 'h' as in 'jalapeno'.

> And no, this phrase is not a tongue twister. It is simply crafted from the words:
> I-ya, i-ya-ha (pronoun for his/hers in Cebuano/Visayan)
> A-ko, a-ko-a (pronoun for mine in Cebuano/Visayan)

Thus,

Iya iya, aku ako.

Which means,

To each his own. (What's hers is hers, what's mine is mine.)

And again, to say it in Boholano, we simply convert the 'y' sound to a 'j' sound.

In addition,
'a-ho' pronounced as /a-hoh/ is the Boholano equivalent for the Visayan word 'ako'.

Example:

If you say,
    'Ako bayang gisakyan ang imong bisekleta.' (I rode your bicycle.)

You can say in Boholano,
    'A-ho bajang gisakjan ang imong bisekleta.'

Again, there are only a few words in Boholano that are distinctly boholano in meaning.

    Boto (of the male sex, in Boholano), Boto (of the female sex, in Cebuano) – Male or Female Genatalia (English)
    Ha-jo (Boholano), La-yo (Cebuano) – Far (English)
    Langas (Boholano), Saba (Cebuano) – Noisy (English)
    Maajong hapon (Boholano), Maayong hapon (Cebuano) – Good afternoon (English)
    Ma-as (Boholano), Tiguwang (Cebuano) – Old (English)
    Ninjo (Boholano), Ninyo (Cebuano) – You/Yours (English)
    Sija (Boholano), Siya (Cebuano) – He/She (English)
    Tangas (Boholano), Labay (Cebuano) – Throw (English)

In closing,
Boholanos say, **'jamo'** *instead of* **'kaayo'** *in Cebuano or* **'very'** *in English.*

Thus,

Lami jamo (Boholano), Lami kaayo (Cebuano) – Very Delicious (English)
Init jamo (Boholano), Init kaayo (Cebuano) – Very Hot (English)

Can you understand what this phrase means? Or at least say it in Cebuano.
Hajo-a man jamo oy!

In Cebuano,
Layo-a man kaayo oy!

In English,
This is quite far.

Chapter 12

Growing Up in the Islands: Lumad nga Bisaya

What is lumad nga Sugbu-anon? Lumad means native, thus, lumad nga Sugbu-anon is a native Cebuano speaker. If Visayan is your native tongue, you are expected to know certain phrases that are only learned from living in the Visayan-speaking islands.

The learning in this chapter is intended for you to get the benefit of speaking and understanding figurative spoken words. To up the ante, the lists that are provided below will put you in the front seat of the Cebuano language learning train.

Figurative Phrases: English to Cebuano

1. At the drop of the hat – en segida, ora mismo, dali kaayo
2. Back to square one – sugod sa uno
3. Beat around the bush – mangulipas
4. Bury the hatchet – kalimtan ang panagbangi
5. Costs an arm and a leg – mahal kaayo
6. Cut corners – magdaginot
7. Feeling a little bit under the weather – magluya
8. Flip one's wig – mag wala; mag huramentado
9. With flying colors – malampuson nga pagkab-ot

10. From the horse's mouth – gikan sa tinubdan
11. Give a dose of one's medicine – patilawon
12. Has no backbone – way baruganan
13. Hit the sack – matulog
14. In leaps and bounds – paspas kaayo
15. It takes two to tango – puros sad-an
16. Let the cat out of the bag – ibutyag
17. Like watching grass grow – pagka-yaya; hinay kaayo
18. Make a long story short – Laktod-saysay; maingon tang punga
19. Miss the boat – giusik ang kahigayonan; napakyas
20. Not a spark of decency – bastos
21. Piece of cake – sayon kaayo; 'chicken!!!'
22. Raining cats and dogs – kusog kaayo nga uwan
23. Sit on the fence – nagduha-duha; nagpanuko
24. Sweet sorrow – makatandog sa kasing-kasing
25. Take the bull by the horns – buntogon; pangis-gan
26. Take with a grain of salt – dili seryosohon; di hatagan ug bili
27. The last straw that broke the camel's back – Ang nakaputong, ang nakahurot sa pailob
28. Weighs a ton – bug-at kaayo
29. Whole nine yards – ang kinatibuk-an
30. Won't be caught dead – Kanus-a pa, Nungka pa

Figurative Phrases: Cebuano to English

1. Ang kalimot way gahum – forgetful
   Literal: Forgetfulness has no will

2. Babaye nga mubo ug lupad – woman of ill-repute
   Literal: A woman who flies low

3. Dili ikapanangpit ang kalami – 7th heaven
   Literal: An ecstasy that can't be shared

4. Gwapa kon magtalikod – homely
   Literal: Beautiful from the backside

5. Humok ug ilong – no conviction; easily swayed

Literal: A soft nose

6. Ikasuroy sa Colon – pretty
   Literal: Can be taken to Colon (a crowded street in Cebu)

7. Ikasuroy sa Colon kon tabunan ug sako – not pretty
   Literal: One who can be paraded in Colon St., only if literally concealed in a sackcloth (sarcasm)

8. Karaang kansyon – an old repeating excuse
   Literal: An old serenade

9. Kulba-hinam – thrilling
   Literal: Nerves-excitement

10. Kung moputi na ang uwak – after a very long time; an impossibility
    Literal: When the black crow turns white

11. La ug dila – one who speaks ill about something or someone, and it happens
    Literal: Has a poisonous tongue

12. Lawom ug dulot – Very serious
    Literal: Cuts deep

13. Magmama ug pula – to have a mouthful of blood after being beaten (a threat)
    Literal: Chew on red

14. Mangkay nga na-ukay – an old maid but who is not necessarily a virgin
    Literal: An old prude that has been deflowered (in olden days, it was taboo for a woman to engage in sex if she was never married, thus, the concept of virginity and being an old unmarried woman were tied together)

15. Mangunay ug silingan – a thief
    Literal: Will take on one's neighbor (originates from the belief that literal witches, will fly far to find a victim rather than take on its own neighbor. It is believed that a thief on the other hand takes no value for respecting and not victimizing a neighbor)

16. Mingaw pa sa Tirana – so quiet
    Literal: More quiet than a melancholic love song

17. Nabiya-an sa tren – an old maid
    Literal: Left behind by the train

18. Nag-aso sa kapungot – very furious
    Literal: Smoking from anger

19. Nagkandila nga grado – grades in straight A
    Literal: Grades that are looking like candles (the Philippine grading system uses 1.0 for A+ in most schools, thus, to get grades in 1s is comparable to seeing a bunch of candles)

20. Nagpaghut sa buwan – asking for the impossible
    Literal: Barking at the moon

21. Nagpangiyod sa kahinam – too excited
    Literal: Humping with excitement

22. Nagpanilap sa tumang kalami – enjoying the deliciousness of something
    Literal: Licking the sides of the mouth to express how tasteful something is

23. Nanubo mora ug uhong – found everywhere; in abundance
    Literal: Sprouting like mushrooms

24. Niguho ang akong kalibutan – I lost all hope
    Literal: My world eroded

25. Nilapas sa kalendaryo – not young anymore
    Literal: Went past the number of days in a calendar month (older than thirty-one)

26. Niputi ang kalimutaw ug hinuwat – took forever to wait
    Literal: One's eyeball turned all white from waiting

27. Panahon ni Mampur – refers to an old era; from way back in time
    Literal: Mampur's time

28. Panas pa sa piso – too flat; too blurry; too unclear
    Literal: Flatter than a one peso coin (in the 1970s, the Philippines used to have 1 peso denomination in coins, and it was typical for some people to play with

it by rubbing it against concrete or a piece of rock until the emblem is flattened and blurred.)

29. Pila'y pad sa unggoy – not discounting anyone's luck
    Literal: How many palms does a monkey have? (this talks about the monkey who is the lowest in the human evolutionary path but still has more than one chance of getting lucky)

30. Taas, gahi ug dako – refer to the qualities of the ideal man
    Literal: Long, hard, and big (a double entundre... why? Foresight, conviction, future ... while playing with someone's imagination)

More Fun With Visayan Tongue Twisters

1. Ang kolor sa purol ni Dolor de kolor.
   Ang kolor – the color
   Purol – boxer shorts
   Dolor – a person's name
   De kolor – multi-colored

2. Ang balay ni Belay libat.
   Ang balay – the house
   Ni – of
   Belay – a person's name
   Libat – cross-eyed

3. Ang relo ni Leroy Rolex.
   Ang relo – the watch
   Ni – of
   Leroy – a person's name
   Rolex – a brand name

4. Ang pugapo namagaybay ug ang bagaybay gipamagaybayan pa gayud.
   Ang pugapo – The 'pugapo' (a kind of fish of the grouper family)

Namagaybay – is oozing with flab
Ug ang bagaybay – and the flab
Gipamagaybayan – is being trimmed with flabby tissue
Pa gayud - still

5. Kuatro ang kwarta ko sa kwadrado nga kwarto.
   Kuatro – four
   Ang kwarta ko – my money
   Kwadrado – square
   Kwarto - room

6. Papa-uli-a si Paula padalhi ug pula nga palwa.
   Papa-uli-a – send home
   Paula – a person's name
   Padal-hi – let her bring
   Pula – red
   Palwa – frond (palm tree branch)

Chapter 13

Distinctly Visayan, Distinctly Filipino

Filipinos in general are a happy people. They live a simple life, and the most miserable ones can't be recognized from their faces since overall, Filipinos have a unique way to humor themselves.

The most telling of these traits perhaps is reflected in the way Cebuano and Visayan people use a convention of naming things especially animals.

The sound that an animal makes can be made as a reference to that animal, Thus,

> Asa ang miming? (Where is the cat?)
> Gipa-ak ko sa aw-aw. (I was bitten by the dog.)
> Naay kokak sa ilawom sa kahoy. (There is a frog under the tree.)
> Ang oink-oink matulog inig kahuman ug kaon. (The pig sleeps after eating.)

These phrases are perfectly valid and understood.

On the contrary, borrowed English words can be crafted to put a funny twist to refer to things.

It's not formally used, but you get to hear phrases like,

Asa ang 'erase da board' (Where is the eraser?)

Ako kang bunalan ining 'sweep da floor' kung di ka mohilom. (I'm going to hit you with this broom, if you don't shut up.)

Again, I would like to emphasize that these are not formal spoken convention but know that when you hear these phrases they are meant to be funny.

Weird Nicknames

For those who have been in these islands for quite a while now, perhaps you also noticed that most people use a moniker of their names by taking a repeated syllable or a modified but still repeated form from the original names.

Hence,

    Che-Che – from Cheryl
    Em-Em – from Emily
    Gong-Gong – from George
    Jojo – from Josephine/Joseph
    Kat-Kat – from Catherine

And you hear aplenty of these nickname conventions anywhere you go.

In line with this, the most recent naming adaptation that perhaps is influenced more by the Western culture, is the opposite of the repetition – the concatenation or shortening of names to have a foreign twist.

Babies that were born in the later years, the millennials, adopt names that are not Filipino sounding anymore, rather the opposite of it.

So, names like,

    Jed – for Joseph Edward
    JP – for John Paul
    LV – Lily Vivienne
    MK – Marie Kristina

I am pointing these things out as part of the evolution of the influence of other cultures on the traditional Filipino or Cebuano (Visayan) people.

Words with Repeated Syllables: The Funny Tongue

Don't be surprised too that the convention of repeating a syllable is rather not sparsely utilized. Can you figure out what these words mean?

Ku-ko
Once in a while, I go to the nail salon to have my 'ku-ko' done.

Bagul-bagol
Your 'bagul-bagol' becomes itchy when you have dandruff.

Dapi-dapi
I got a serious bruise on my right 'dapi-dapi' after I fell, that is why I'm leaning with my left bottom when I sit.

Bul-bol
In some culture, shaving the 'bul-bol' is taboo.

Suk-sok
She wouldn't take the money so I 'suk-sok' it in her pocket when she wasn't watching.

Luk-lok
Drug dealers have the ability to 'luk-lok' the drugs in places where they can't be easily found.

Tad-tad
It's so hard to 'tad-tad' the meat with a dull knife.

Duk-dok
You need a hammer if you want to 'duk-dok' this nail down.

Su-so
In some countries, it is perfectly acceptable for a woman to expose her 'su-so' to breastfeed her child.

Ok-ok
Among the flying insects the 'ok-ok' is probably one of the dirtiest and nastiest.

Ba-ba
When I told her the truth, her 'ba-ba' opened wide in disbelief.

Sing-sing
Oh, so you love her? Then put a 'sing-sing' on it.

Bot-bot
I can't believe anything you say. Your either lying or making them up. You're so full of 'bot-bot.'

Pang-pang
Our vehicle almost fell down the 'pang-pang' when we lost control of the steering wheel.

Ka-ka
This 'ka-ka' is called the black widow because it is so poisonous and deadly.

Ang-ang
When you go up and down the stairs, be mindful of each 'ang-ang'.

Ung-ong
Do not 'ung-ong' by the door. Either you go in, or you stay outside.

Huna-huna
I can't sleep at night because you are always in my 'huna-huna.'

Kasing-kasing
Everytime I see you, my 'kasing-kasing' skips a beat.

Duha-duha
I'm still in a state of 'duha-duha'. I don't know what to do.

Bung-bong
I want this 'bung-bong' to be painted white so this room will look bigger.

Tung-tong
Oh, please do not 'tung-tong' your feet on the table when you read the paper.

Double the Words, Double the Fun

And lastly, certain verbs can be manipulated to mean a past progressive event.

Nagtuyok-tuyok man mi. (We were circling around.)
(Root word: tuyok/to turn around)

Nagsuroy-suroy mi sa parke. (We were leisurely walking in the park.)
(Root word: Suroy/to stroll)

Ang bata nagsaka-saka sa hagdan. (The child was playfully climbing up the stairs.)
(Root word: saka/to climb)

Nagkanta-kanta mi ganiha didto sa videoke-han. (We were singing earlier at the videoke bar.) (Root word: kanta/to sing)

Nagsunod-sunod siya kanako, nga mora'g itoy. (He was following me like a puppy.)
(Root word: sunod/to follow)

Naglangoy-langoy mi sa dagat gahapon. (We were swimming at sea yesterday.)
(Root word: langoy/to swim)

Ang dalan nagliku-liko. (The road is winding.)
(Root word: liko/to take turn; baliko/curved)

So, what is the difference if we don't repeat the word?

Nagtuyok man mi. (The meaning is altered.) (Nituyok man mi, is better.)

Nagsuroy mi sa parke. (Misuroy mi sa parke, is more grammatically apt.)

Ang bata nisaka sa hagdan. (Same but more of a declarative approach.)

Nagkanta mi ganiha didto sa karaoke-han. (Same but doesn't sound fun.)

Nagsunod siya kanako nga mora ug itoy. (Same but a more serious tone.)

Naglangoy mi sa dagat gahapon. (Same but doesn't seem fun.)

Ang dalan nagliko. (Awkward, since 'nagliko' means 'taking a turn'.)

In most cases, the context is not lost, but in some exceptions, it can also change the meaning of the phrase.

    Nagtuyok man mi. - 'We are spinning.'

As opposed to,

    Nagtuyok-tuyok man mi. – 'We were circling around.'

Perhaps the most notable change is that, when these phrases are spoken without repeated verb, the air of fun or the tone of a 'leisurely activity' or a 'continuous' or 'progressive event' denoted by the phrase is eliminated. It is fair to assume that the narrative sounds more serious and less pleasant now compared to the original statements.

Repeating the words in a verb could be either of these three things:
- To denote a fun event or activity
- To denote a less serious tone to a narrative
- To mean doing a 'little bit of this' and 'a little bit of that'

Sometimes these repeated phrases are implicitly expressed as they are:

    Nagkaon-kaon mi ganiha.
    Nagkanta-kanta mi gabii.

Is tantamount to saying,

    Nagkalingaw ug kaon mi ganiha.
    Nagkalingaw ug kanta mi gabii.

Lingaw in Cebuano or Visayan is 'fun' or 'being amused'.

Chapter 14

21st Century Visayan Adaptation

This is the part where we take the litmus test of how much bilingual expansion have we gained from learning and immersing ourselves in the lessons from the previous chapters. Have we armed ourselves enough? Let's find out.

Do you have a better translation?

Artificial intelligence – Salingkapaw nga salabutan
Athletic performance – Katakos sa paugnat sa kusog
Binge-watch – Way puas nga pagtan-aw
Business development – Kalambuan sa negosyo
Carbon footprint – Karbon nga namugna sa matag proseso
Change agent – Ahente sa pagbag-o
Cognitive research – Kognitibong panukiduki
Consumer engagement – Siguristang pag-agni sa konsumante
Emoji – Nagkadaiyang simbolo sa pagkighinabi
Emoticon – Sinyas nga pang-emosyon
Engaging design – Makadani nga desenyo
Global competence – Katakos nga makig-indig sa tibuok kalibutan
Historic preservation – Makasaysayanong pag-preserbar
Re-imagined luxury – Ginabag-o nga alindog
Sesquipedalian – Puno sa mga pulong
SMH – Tsk tsk tsk
Tourism – Turismo
YOLO – Kausa ra ka mabuhi

The Electronic Domain and The Social Media

1. *Activity* log – Lista sa *gipanggama*
2. Add a *contact* – Magdugang ug *ka-ila*
3. *Additional tabs* menu – Lista nga kapilian sa *dugang nga mga panid*
4. *Apps* – Mga *programadong galamiton* alang sa pang elektronikong himan o hiramenta
5. *Ask for* recommendations – *Mangayo ug mga* rekomendasyon
6. Block *settings* – *Lagda* sa pagbabag
7. *Blocking* – Mga *gipangbabagan* ug *gusto nga babagan*
8. *Change* Phone Number – *Usabon* ang numero sa telepono
9. *Chat* – *Makig-hinabi*
10. *Verify* the SMS on your *phone to complete the sign-up process* – *Suta-a* ang mensahe sa imong mobilo nga telepono *aron makompleto ang proseso sa pag-apil*
11. *Comment* – *Mosuwat ug komento*
12. Connect to *email-provider* – modugtong sa *tigpasiugda sa imong pang elektronikong suwat*
13. *Contact* Number – Numero *diin pwede ka ma-abot*
14. *Cookies* Settings – Lagda sa *tigtima-an ug tighinumdom sa mga suok nga imong gibisita ug nahikaplagan sa wanang sa elektronikong kalihokan*
15. Create *fundraiser* – Magpasiugda ug *pagpa-usbaw sa salapi alang sa maayong katuyo-an*
16. *Create* Group – *Magmugna* ug grupo
17. Create new *slideshow* – Maghimo ug bag-ong *pasundayag sa mga hinugpong nga pahina*
18. *Create* page – *Maghimo ug bag-ong* pahina
19. *Download* a **copy** of *your data* – *Mohupot* ug **hulad** sa *gipanag-iya nimo nga datos*
20. Drop *link* – i-dugang ang *kutay sa pahina sa wanang nga elektroniko*
21. *Edit* settings and features – *Mani-obrahon* ang mga lagda ug mga aspeto
22. *Expand* Video – *Padak-on* ang bidyo

23. _Explore_ – _Magduki-duki_
24. _Face_ recognition – Pag-ila sa _hitsura_
25. Find _friends_ - mangita ug mga _higala_
26. Follow _requests_ – Mga hangyo nga mosunod
27. Help friends _find more_ – Tabangi ang mga higala nga _maka-kaplag pa ug dugang_
28. _Inbox_ – elektronikong kahon sa mga mapahimuslanong suwat ug pahibalo nga nadawat
29. Jump _to_ – Ambak _ngadto sa_
30. _Landing_ page – _tugpahanan_ nga pahina
31. _Language_ – _Linggwahe_
32. _Like_ this page – _Hi-uyoni_ kini nga pahina
33. _Live_ Video – _Kasamtangang_ kalihokan nga gisikop sa bidyo-kamera
34. _Manage_ settings – _mani-obrahon_ ang mga lagda
35. _Market_place – lugar k_omprahanan_
36. More _options_ – dugang nga _mga kapili-an_
37. _Navigate_ to – _mo-adto_ sa
38. Newsfeed _Preferences_ – _na-uyonan nga lagda_ sa mga madawat nga pang-elektronikong balita
39. _On this day_ – (mga panghitabo) _ni-ining adlawa_
40. Open _attachment_ – abrihi ang _pataban sa suwat_
41. _Please_ enter a _valid e-mail address_ or mobile number – _palihug_ ug butang ug _balido nga padad-anan sa elektronikong suwat_ o numero sa mobilo nga telepono
42. _Press_ home to unlock – _Pindota_ ang butones nga <home> aron maabri ang elektronikong kandado
43. _Privacy_ – lagda sa _pribadong katungod_
44. Public _posts_ -Pang-publiko nga _gipangmantala nga kalihokan_
45. Security and _login_ – Seguridad ug lagda sa _pagdayon_
46. See _more_ – Motan-aw pa ug _dugang_
47. _Share_ – _ipa-ambit_ sa uban
48. _Temperature_ – _lagda sa kainiton o kabugnawon_
49. _Tagging_ – giya sa _pagpatik_ sa mga kaila
50. _Unfollow_ – _talikdan_, undangon ang pagpakighigala ug biyaan

Chapter 16

Hashtag in Cebuano, Anyone?

From #Artless to #Zizz

n this age of Instagram, Facebook, Twitter, newsfeeds, blogs, and the like, the hashtag is an invaluable tool in wrangling data for ease, mind you. In case you are not aware, it helps power analytics to help decode your digital DNA.

(<u>Sa panahon karon</u> sa Instagram, Facebook, Twitter, <u>elektronikong balita</u>, <u>elektronikong mga sinulat</u>, <u>ug susama nga mga butang</u>, ang 'hashtag' <u>usa ka bililhon nga galamiton sa paggutad-gutad sa mga datos sa tumang kasayon</u>, <u>abi mo lang</u>. <u>Kana kung wala ka masayud</u>, <u>mitabang kini sa pagpasiugda sa pagtino ug pagbasa sa mga datos aron masayran ug masabtan ang imong kalihokan sa wanang sa kompyuter ug sa internet</u>.)

How do you even say hashtag in Cebuano (Visayan)? I can tell you that this word, albeit, new, is simply a modern twist to an old way of marking documents manually.

A hashtag is like an index or a marker or some systematic coded words to identify a group of information online.

Thus, hashtag could be translated as
'tima-an' – marker
Or
'indise' – a borrowed word for 'index'
Or
'sumbananan nga pulong' – reference word
Or
'giya nga pulong' – guide word

Can you think of another translation?

Check the following hashtags. The hashtags in Cebuano are longer. A basic understanding of the Cebuano vocabulary is required together with a good set of bifocals, so you can slice and dice the Visayan words with ease.

Can you provide an alternate hashtag in Cebuano?

I hear an unequivocal, YES.

#amazingplanet
#mabulukonngaplaneta
(mabulukon nga planeta)

#beautifuldestinations
#mgamaanindotngadestinasyon
(mga maanindot nga destinasyon)

#couplegoals
#pangandoysamagtiayon
(pangandoy sa magtiayon)

#dreamcatchers
#tigsawosamgadamgo
(tigsawo sa mga damgo)

#everygirlsdream
#damgosamatagbabaye
(damgo sa matag babaye)

#forevergrateful
#mapasalamatonhangtudsakahangturan
(mapasalamaton hangtud sa kahangturan)

#godisgoodallthetime
#angGinoomaayosatanangpanahon
(ang Ginoo maayo sa tanang panahon)

#heavenisaplaceonearth
#anglangitusakalugarsakalibutan
(ang langit usa ka lugar sa kalibutan)

#iammybrotherskeeper
#akoangmagbalantaysaakongigsoon
(ako ang magbalantay sa akong igsoon)

#justwhatineeded
#angakogyud nga gikinahanglan
(ang ako gyud nga gikinahanglan)

#keepingitreal
#pagpabilinniiningamatinud-anon
(pagpabilin niini nga matinud-anon)

#keepingthefaith
#paghangopsapagtuo
(paghangop sa pagtuo)

#livetheliteyoulove
#puyiangkinabuhingaimonggihigugma
(puy-i ang kinabuhi nga imong gihigugma)

#mykindothappy
#angmatangsaakongkalipay
(ang matang sa akong kalipay)

#nothinglikefamily
#walaysusamasapamilya
(walay susama sa pamilya)

#onelifeliveit
#usakakinabuhipuyikini
(usa ka kinabuhi, puy-i kini)

#peoplewhodofunstuff
#mgatawongamobuhatuglingawngamgabutang
(mga tawo nga mibuhat ug lingaw nga mga butang)

#qualitytime
#orasngadekalidad
(oras nga de kalidad)

#roamtheplanet
#suroyonangplaneta
(suroyon ang planeta)

#sunrisesunsetsaroundtheworld
#pagsidlakugpagsawopsaadlawsatibuokkalibutan
(pagsidlak ug pagsawop sa adlaw sa tibuok kalibutan)

#trysomethingdifferenteveryday
#suwayianglaingbutangmatagadlaw
(suwayi ang laing butang matag adlaw)

#underthesamesky
#sailawomsaparehongalangit
(sa ilawom sa pareho nga langit)

#visitBohol
#bisitahaangBohol
(bisitaha ang Bohol)

#workoutmotivation
#pagagnisapagehersisyo
(pag-agni sa pag-ehersisyo)

#xoxo
#halokgakoshalokgakos
(halok gakos halok gakos)

#yestowellness
#oosamaayongpanglawas
(oo sa maayong panglawas)

#zerowastelifestyle
#wayusikngapaagisapagpuyosakinabuhi
(way usik nga paagi sa pagpuyo sa kinabuhi)

Chapter 17

Makagagahum or Gamhanan?

Which one are you?

or a Cebuano or Visayan makagagahum is the alternate word for Ginoo – God

If I say,
    Ang labaw nga makagagahum maga-uban kaninyo!

That is tantamount to saying,
    The most powerful on high will guide you!

That is also the reason why the shortened term 'gamhanan' is more apt to use to create an opinion of power about someone.

'Gamhanan' though could be used as a mockery to someone who exercises absolute power in any setting.

Say,
    Gamhanan kaayo ka da!
    Di gyud ka pa-lupig sa istorya.

Almost certainly would mean,
    You are too much
    You don't let others talk.

If someone would say,
    Oy pagkagamhanan gyud sa akong anak.
    Numero uno siya sa klase.

It is used to praise someone's excellence,
> Oh my, my child is so amazing!
> He is number one in his class.

Once in a while, you will hear the context of 'makagagahum' out of the Godly designation, like if someone says, '*ang mga makakagahum sa gobyerno*' and it's perfectly valid to mean, '*the authority in the government*'.

Or '*ang makagagahum nga tagdumala sa nasud*' which is the country's president.

Going back to the word *gamhanan*, it can also be used to refer to a non-person to express intensity of influence.

Say,
> *Gamhanan kaayo ang akong eskwelahan.*
> *Bisan kon nagbagyo, nagklase gihapon.*

Translation:
> My school is unbelievable.
> Even if there is typhoon, classes are still being held.

Or
> *Gamhanan kaayo ang barko nga akong gisakyan.*
> *Bisan napuno na, naa gihapoy gipasakay nga walay tiket.*

Translation:
> The boat that I took is beyond crazy.
> Even if it was already full, there were still those without ticket that were allowed to go on board.

Or
> *Gamhanan kaayo ka ba.*
> *Di ka mouli kung dili tungang gabii.*

Translation:
> You are out of control.
> You don't come home not unless it's midnight.

Or
> *Gamhanan kaayo ang imong baho.*

Makalipong!

Translation:
> Your body odor is unbearable.
> It's dizzying.

Or

Unsay pagtuo nimo? Ingon ana ka kagamhanan?

Translation:
> What do you think? You are that powerful?

Now you see that this word could essentially mean anything depending on how it is used in the context of other words and phrases.

And this holds true for most words that have no definite word translation or for words that are derived from other words, in this case 'gahum' – power.

The one thing that I wish to point out as the most obvious usage of this word is what I intended it to be used for – to denote achievement of a remarkable feat. What's so remarkable? The attempt to further your learning experience of the Cebuano (Visayan) dialect; that is remarkable.

So, this is the point where I will gladly say to you,

Gamhanan gyud ka.

Imo gayud nga natuhog ang mga pagtulon-an mahitungod sa pagkat-on sa pinulongang Sugbuanon ug Bisaya. Mapasalamaton ug mapasigarbohon ako nga motamod kanimo isip usa ka takos nga ehemplo sa usa ka tawo nga nagmadaugon sa iyang paningkamot nga masabtan ang pinulongang Bisaya.

Ug busa, ako ikaw nga pahinumdoman sa gidak-on sa imong nakab-ot nga kalampusan tungod kay dili sayon ang pagkat-on ug bag-o nga pinulongan.

Ug ayaw kalimti nga ang pinakasayon nga paagi sa pagkat-on sa pinulongang Bisaya mao ang kanunay nga paghubad sa mga pulong nga Ingles ngadto sa pulong nga Sugbuanon inabagan sa imong nakat-onan ug posible usab, uban ang usa ka kasaligan nga diksyonaro sa mga pulong nga Ingles ug Sugbuanon.

Kung kanunay kini nimong pagabuhaton, akong ikapaniguro kanimo nga sa di halayong panahon, tuman nimo nga masabtan bisan ang mga pinakalisud nga mga pulong. Ug dili nimo ika-hadlok ang pagsuway sa pag lakbit sa mga pulong nga Binisaya.

Mainiton nga pagdayeg sa imong kalamposan!

In closing remember these phrases:

We create our interpretations out of our past experiences.
Atong gimugna ang atong mga interpretasyon gikan sa mga kanhi-ay nato nga mga naagi-an sa kinabuhi.

And since we have different life experiences,
Ug tungod kay lain-lain kita ug naagi-an sa kinabuhi,

No two people will also have the same interpretations.
Wala usa'y duha ka tawo nga pareho ug pagsabot sa tanang butang.

In parting,

"If you want happiness for an hour, take a nap.
Kung gusto ka ug kalipay alang sa usa ka oras, pag tagpilaw.

If you want happiness for a day, go fishing.
Kung gusto ka ug kalipay alang sa usa ka adlaw, adto pa-ngisda.

If you want happiness for a year, inherit a fortune.
Kung gusto ka ug kalipay alang sa usa ka tuig, pa-nunod ug bahandi.

If you want happiness for a lifetime, help somebody.
Kung gusto ka ug kalipay alang sa tibuok kinabuhi, tabangi ang usa ka tawo."

Panultihong Intsik
(Chinese Proverb)

I hope this book has helped you.
Hinaut nga kining basahon nakatabang kanimo.

Sa kinahiladman sa akong kasing-kasing,
From the bottom of my heart,

Palihug dawata ang akong mainiton nga pagpasalamat kanimo.
Please accept my warmest gratitude to you.

Daghan kaayong Salamat!

Made in the USA
San Bernardino, CA
11 July 2018